52 Weeks to Well-Being:

What a Woman Needs to Know to Become Queen of Her Finances

Peggy Doviak

CENTERBOARD PRESS

Centerboard Press
Norman, Oklahoma

Printed in the United States | First Edition May 2023

Library of Congress Control Number: 2023908336

For information on orders: peggy@peggydoviak.com

Names: Doviak, Peggy
Title: 52 weeks to well-being: what a woman needs to know to become queen
of her finances / by Peggy Doviak
Other Titles: 52 weeks to well-being
Description: First edition | Norman, Oklahoma: Centerboard Press
Identifiers: ISBN 979-8-218-20438-9
Subjects: LCSH: Finance, Personal. | Wealth. | Taxation. | Financial Planning.

10 9 8 7 6 5 4 3 2 1

Disclaimer

The information in this book is educational in nature and not investment advice. Consult any strategy with your own financial team before you implement it. Investing is risky, and you can lose money.

Additionally, any time the terms "financial planner" or "planner" are used, the assumption is the author is referring to a CERTIFIED FINANCIAL PLANNER™ practitioner.

To Richard—forever my love, forever my muse.

Contents

Timeline of American Women and Finance

Date	Event	Founder/Owner
2020	First Treasury Secretary	Janet L. Yellen
2018	First Female Head of the New York Stock Exchange	Stacey Cunningham
2014	First Female Chair of Federal Reserve	Janet L. Yellen
2009	Lilly Ledbetter Fair Pay Act	
1988	Women's Business Ownership Act	
1974	Equal Credit Opportunity Act	
1972	First woman CEO of a Fortune 500 company	Katharine Graham
1967	Affirmative action benefits expanded to include women	
1963	First "equal pay for equal work" legislation	
1920	19th Amendment granted white women the right to vote	
1919	First Women's Bank of Tennessee for women customers only	
1880	Stock exchange opened for women who want to use own money to speculate on railroad and mining stocks	Mary Gage
1870	Sisters open a Wall Street brokerage firm	Victoria Woodhull Tennessee Claflin
1869	First American woman who drafts prenup before she remarries	Lydia Moss Bradley
1865	First real woman to be featured on currency	Pocahontas
1848	Married Woman's Property Act	
1809	First woman to hold a patent in her name	Mary Kies
1639	First Puritan divorce	Elizabeth Luxford

Introduction

I never intended to write a financial book designed for women; however, I've found most of the existing books less than exciting. The financial services industry has created an amazing amount of nonsense designed specifically for their female clients. Their typical message is, "We're aware you don't know very much about money. Don't fret about it, honey. We will explain just enough of the basics, so you can feel confident trusting us to make the complicated decisions for you." If their pieces of paper could pat you on the head, they would.

This book takes a different perspective. If you don't know a lot about money, that's okay. We're going to start at the beginning. But then, once we have addressed basic issues, we're going to look at more complicated problems. How do you start a business? What resources exist for women caught in the sandwich of caring for children and aging parents at the same time? How do you make good financial decisions if you are recently widowed or divorced? How do you ask for a raise? In short, how can you manage your finances in an empowered way?

To address these issues, the book is divided into fifty-two short chapters. Your goal is to read one a week and address the "next steps" at the end of each of them. After the year, you won't need to put blind trust in anyone. You will know enough about your financial world to make your own decisions or work wisely with your financial team. No one gets a pat on their head in this book!

I believe it's important for women to understand their money, because understanding your money takes power away from others and gives it back to you! Today, many of us choose to stay single or find ourselves unexpectedly single through divorce or being widowed. Because of these situations, most women will be the only financial decision maker for at least part of their lives. But don't be afraid.

I wrote this book to give you confidence. I'm surprised how many women are quick to let their spouse or partner take the lead in their finances. I'm always horrified when a woman who is otherwise capable, confident, or well educated tells me that she's "just not a number's person" and leaves it up to the man.

I'm going to let you in on a little secret—for years I didn't define myself as a "number's person" either. My first master's degree was in Creative Studies, and my thesis was a collection of short stories! When I wrote my dissertation, I used to laugh and say that my research was so qualitative that I wouldn't have numbered the pages if they hadn't made me. But then, I changed careers and needed to learn about numbers and money.

If I can do it, you can too! Of course, I had strong motivation. In the 1960s, my mother was the salutatorian and the only woman in her MBA graduating class from Washington University. She was offered a seat on the Chicago Board of

Trade but didn't want that much stress. At fifty, she took her CPA exam and passed it on the first try with the second highest grade in the state. In her job, she conducted international tax audits for a major oil company with extensive overseas holdings.

When my crazy-smart, capable mother retired, she rolled her 401(k) into an IRA, and let a stockbroker manage her investments. She let him know she wanted to make money, so he put her rollover account into high tech single stocks in March 2000 without thinking about her age or risk tolerance. She was a genius at accounting but knew virtually nothing about the stock market. She went on to lose 40% of her account's value due to risky investments that never regained their value.

I began to study, trying to determine what had happened to Mom, as I also knew nothing about the stock market. The more I read, the madder I became. By 2003, I had opened my own financial firm so no one else would have the same condescending, self-serving treatment that my mother experienced at the hands of the broker. I went on to earn my CERTIFIED FINANCIAL PLANNER™ (CFP®) designation, completing a comprehensive curriculum of financial topics. I'll talk more about designations in Chapter Twelve.

Twenty years after that life-changing event, I've written a book for you—another smart, savvy woman who would like a little financial information presented in a way that isn't mind numbing. To help with that I've included new "friends" who will be joining us—women who may have stories similar to yours. Further, each chapter starts with a personal experience of someone in my world and concludes with next steps you can take. This is a book filled with real world situations and solutions. I'm excited to be with you on this journey. I'll be staying with you, as well, by updating information on my website, www.askpeggy.com. And remember, if you have a question, you can always submit it on the site, as well. Let's get started!

Meet Our Friends

MEGAN is in her early twenties. She is a single mom raising a three-year-old girl named Charlotte. She married just out of high school, and her marriage lasted until shortly after Charlotte was born. Megan wants to earn her associate's degree, but she works two jobs with varying shifts. Money is tight, and she struggles to pay her bills. She wants to gain control of her financial situation.

JESSICA is in her thirties. She has an excellent job in her field, and she wants to climb in the company. She's not opposed to a relationship, but she wants to focus more on her career rather than starting a family. Some of her friends understand her ambition, but others don't. She also worries that because she is young, she isn't taken as seriously as she would be if she were older ... or male.

KIM is in her early fifties, and has been in a long-term relationship with her partner, Sam. She has a good job in an IT department, but she doesn't find it inspiring. She really wants to start her own computer consulting business. Sam works but doesn't earn a lot of money. They know they will need to plan carefully if Kim makes a career change.

SHARON is a sixty-something-year-old widow. No one knows her age, as she won't admit it. Her husband died last year. Although she thinks he left her financially stable, she doesn't want to make mistakes, and she has been dodging calls every week from financial professionals who want to "help." She's afraid they really just want to help themselves to her money. She knows she's lucky that her kids have financial stability, but she doesn't want to be a burden on them. She wants to stay in her own home as she ages, and she worries about how much that will cost.

What You Need to Know

Hetty Green: The Witch of Wall Street

EVEN IF YOU have no interest in the stock market, you may have heard of Warren Buffett. Buffett is the modern-day stock market genius praised for his focus on long-term investing in companies that are currently in a slump. His approach is called "value investing," but nearly a hundred years before Buffett, Hetty Green was innovating the same strategy.

Hetty was born into a family made wealthy by whaling and shipping, and she inherited the gene. After being rejected by her father for having the audacity not to be a boy, she was encouraged by her grandfather to understand financial concepts. By the age of eight, she opened a bank account, and by thirteen, she was the accountant for the family business. She cared little about traditional "female" interests and sold a wardrobe purchased by her father to attract a suitor. She then used the money to purchase government bonds.

Hetty eventually did get married to Edward Henry Green but required her future husband to sign a pre-nup agreement. Through inherited money and her own investing skills, she was already a wealthy woman. She invested in real estate and stocks and continued to buy the bonds she appreciated as a teen. Although Edward was also an investor, he was not as successful as his wife, and three times she had to cover his debts. The third time in 1885, she left him, although they did not divorce. By this time, Hetty Green was called the "Queen of Wall Street." Her value investing strategy caused her to prosper often when others were struggling, and eventually her moniker changed from "queen" to "witch." The witch reputation was the result of jealousy and Hetty's practice of wearing Victorian black after Edward died. She furthered her unique reputation by using little hot water or heat, eating inexpensive foods, and avoiding medical treatment.

Her phrase, "Watch your pennies and the dollars will take care of themselves," is still commonly given advice. When she died, the *New York Times* wrote that had Hetty Green been a man, her concern with finance and financial gain would have been considered normal. However, women weren't encouraged to be materialistic. When she died in 1916, with a net worth of one hundred to two hundred million dollars, Hetty Green was with little doubt the richest woman in America. Today that would be two to four billion dollars! Rather than considering her a witch, we should remember her as her last nickname, the "Wizard of Wall Street."

Chapter 1

Look Up—Be Brave

The woman in my office looked down and wouldn't meet my gaze. She twisted and untwisted the tissue in her hand as she told me that she felt like a financial failure. She knew she hadn't made great financial decisions, and she didn't know where to start. She interviewed another financial adviser before our meeting, and he just tried to get her to open an investment account. She felt like that wasn't where she should start. She hoped I would offer a different perspective.

MY BUSINESS HAD BEEN open for about a month when the woman came into my office. As the meeting progressed, I was glad she had brought her own tissue. I didn't have any tissues in my office, and I panicked when she started crying.

I didn't have any financial training in how to deal with a crying client, so I just promised her that I would help her create a plan. I assured her that we would work through everything and come up with solutions. I know. I should have added a disclaimer to that promise, but she was crying. I decided on the spot that we WOULD come up with a solution.

Since then, I've bought tissues, because although she was the first to cry in my office, she certainly hasn't been the last. It's a human reaction—when we feel overwhelmed and hopeless, we show emotion.

So we are going to begin here. If you are panicking about your money, you're in the right place. If you are ashamed, know that there isn't any judgment in this book. Look up. Be brave. Figure out where you are financially, and then you can create a solution.

Where do you begin? I believe that the only way to create a workable plan is to know where you are financially. To make this possible, I want you to begin by tracking what you spend each month. I don't care how you log your spending—whether it's a phone app, a notebook, or your laptop. I want you to write down every single thing you buy, no matter how small, and I don't want you to judge yourself while you do it. Additionally, it's not just you. Everyone in your household should participate. Include your spouse or partner and any children. Everyone should write down their spending, however insignificant it is.

We're going to use this data for many things, including how to get out of debt, create an emergency fund, determine your retirement needs, and evaluate life insurance. These exercises will fall apart if you don't know how much you and your family spend.

At the end of the month, I want you to categorize your expenses, so "utilities" would be a category, as would "groceries," "rent," "car payments," "eating out," etc. Some of your categories will be fixed, while other groupings could be adjusted if needed. If you shop at a super store, try to break your bill between household needs, groceries, and items you just wanted.

If you're like most people, you will look at the categories

at the end of the month and tell me that this month wasn't truly representative of what you usually spend. Okay. Then just to be sure, I want you to track your spending for a second month, or maybe even a third.

Additionally, you will want to take holidays, birthdays, and vacations into account. These costs only occur periodically, and they can be overlooked. You want your cash flow analysis to be accurate.

Having a clear image of how much you spend, even if it's higher than you would like, can be freeing. Now you know where you are. With this knowledge, you no longer have to fear your money. No more tears. No looking down. You can begin to prosper.

Megan: I already track most of my spending because I have to do it. I can't run out of money before pay day.

Jessica: I like to track my expenses on my phone. When I use an app, it's easy to write down everything as I purchase it or pay a bill.

Kim: Before Peggy told me it was the basis of everything, I didn't think I needed to track my spending. Everything would change if I decided to open my own business. I will need to know how much money I needed to earn to cover our expenses.

Sharon: I'm so old school. I like to use ledger paper to write down what I spend, and I keep it up every month.

Next Steps:

Track your family's spending for one or more months until you know your monthly recurring costs, discretionary purchases, vacation and holiday spending, along with any other categories. Use the following lines to jot down any notes.

_____

_____

_____

_____

_____

_____

_____

_____

_____

Chapter 2

Budgets That Work

A woman came into my office believing she was in serious financial trouble. As I listened to her story, I agreed. She had lost a good job with a pension and benefits and had taken an hourly position just to bring in some money. She was drowning in debt but didn't want to declare bankruptcy. She thought she could work her way out of it. When she asked me what to do, I told her that she needed to track her spending. Then, we could try to create a budget for her current income level. If she had sufficient resources to pay her bills, even with a few spending modifications, then she would have more options.

ONCE YOU KNOW how much money you are spending each month, you can create a budget that helps you categorize your costs using real data. I believe that budgets fail for two major reasons. First, we believe that our budget has more power over us than it does. We're afraid of our budgets, and when we fail to keep them, we run from them. Then, our spending falls completely apart. The second reason we avoid our budgets is because we make them with unrealistic numbers.

Most people don't ever honestly track their spending, and

as a result, budgets are created using estimated numbers. After the activity in the first chapter, you may have discovered that if you estimated your spending, you guessed too low!

I suspect this is true because I also completed the cash flow exercise when I was contemplating quitting my previous job and moving full time into my financial planning practice. I knew the decision would require us to depend more on my husband's salary, so we tracked our spending for a month. I didn't believe how much we ate out, so we tracked it for a second month. Then I learned how to cook!

If you completed the first chapter, you have the information you need to create your family budget. If you have sufficient resources to pay your bills and save enough for retirement and any future major costs, like college, then your budget is simply plugging in the appropriate numbers. But many of us find creating a budget more difficult.

You know the premise of a budget—list your income each month, categorize your expenses, and deduct them from your income. Any remaining money is what you use to create an emergency fund, additional retirement savings, investment accounts, or even vacations and gifts. Yes, I've heard you're supposed to pay yourself first, but not getting evicted is probably a higher priority. Usually, I find people pay their primary bills and then use the additional money for savings. If you don't have additional money or even have more bills than income, then you need to look for places where you can cut expenses.

This is one of the first places where financial planning becomes a family activity. Obviously, if you have more expenses than income, something's got to go. Nondiscretionary expenses are hard to adjust, so first you will want to look at your discretionary spending habits. If you have to choose between a cheaper cell phone plan or fewer cable television channels, you can take a family vote. If you need to eat out less, create a family meal prep plan. Even younger children enjoy setting the table or helping with safe tasks. Older teens might enjoy being allowed to plan and prepare a meal of their choosing.

Spending less money isn't a punishment; it should be seen as a challenge. Have a family contest to see who can spend the least amount over the course of the month—with a modest prize for the winner, of course.

You're accomplishing two things with this activity. First, obviously, you are spending less. But secondly, and maybe even more importantly, you are seeing how you can be in control of your money. You are making it fun to save. And as a result, you are removing the fear from the budget process.

We fail at money decisions largely because we are so afraid of them that we don't take a good look at our situation. When you track your spending, build a budget from that data, use available funds for savings or major purchases, and make any adjustments you need to stay in balance. Then, you are absolutely on the road to prosperity!

Megan: I just hate looking at my finances because it's so stressful. I need to stop being afraid and create a plan.

Jessica: I know I have some money left at the end of each month. I need to look more closely at my cash flow and decide how to use that surplus without just spending it.

Kim: I want to look at our spending now, while we still have enough money, so we have a plan when I branch out.

Sharon: I have many recurring subscriptions for newspapers, services, and magazines. I don't read half of them and bet I wouldn't miss them. There's no point spending money on something I don't use.

Next Steps

Create a budget from your cash flow exercise in the last chapter. Remember to include columns for an emergency fund and retirement savings—topics we will address in future weeks. You can jot notes on the following lines.

Chapter 3

Saving for Emergencies

When I speak to a group, I'll often ask the room how many people have saved an emergency fund. A few hands always go up, but many don't. When I ask people if they could save a six-month emergency fund, they laugh.

"No." "Not hardly." "Are you kidding?" are common responses. Then, they all begin to look at me nervously, afraid of what I am going to say next. The room visibly relaxes when I smile and tell them it's okay. I'm going to make it easy.

I THINK MOST personal finance celebrities don't understand the lives of real people. For example, from the safe side of the radio or television, some will tell you that all debt is bad, and you can't even THINK about a family vacation until your home is paid off. Others will sit back and tell you that you don't have enough money to achieve the goal or dream you shared with them.

But that's not all. With no guidance on how to accomplish their directive, they will tell you that you need a six-month emergency fund to cover expenses in case you lose your job. Six months? To many people, the task seems impossible.

COVID-19 solidified my belief in the importance of a large emergency fund. I was horrified at how many people, who appeared to have safe employment, suddenly couldn't work. And yet, some of the advice on how to create the fund can be overwhelming.

Instead of that, let me help you create an emergency fund in a way you can sustain. First, why do you need an emergency fund? Even without a pandemic, life happens. Your job may be secure, but your car can quit running, your kid breaks his arm, and water can start coming out of unexpected places in your dishwasher all on the same day!

What do you do? Research suggests that most Americans couldn't pay an unexpected $700 bill. As a result, most people pull out a little piece of plastic. Then, at the end of the month, they pay the minimum balance, and the debt begins to increase. Now, I'm not opposed to using credit cards, but you should try very hard to pay them off each month. When you use the card to cover a spate of crises, it's likely you won't be able to do that.

An emergency fund could help you in this situation. Technically, the funds are designed to cover nondiscretionary expenses in case you lose your job, but they can cover unexpected disasters too.

How much money should you keep in reserve? I promised you I'm not going to overwhelm you at first with six months. Instead, to determine how much money you need to save, we'll look at your information from the first chapter. What was your average monthly nondiscretionary spending? Remember that nondiscretionary spending is for those bills you must pay each month to survive. Take this amount and multiply it by six to get the total amount of the emergency fund that it would be nice to have.

If I left it here, I wouldn't be any better than the people I was talking about earlier in the chapter. To avoid being unrealistic, rather than multiplying your monthly spending by six, I want you to divide it by two. Yes, divide it; don't multiply it. Look at that number. If you focused on saving that much money, do you think you could do it over the next six months? Nine months? Year? I'll bet you can!

Even if you're not confident, try moving a small amount of money automatically from your existing bank account to a new one at the beginning of the month. Your new account should be a savings account without an ATM card attached to it. The money is available, but you have to literally walk into the bank to access it.

By moving the money automatically, you won't be inclined to skip your deposit in the difficult months. Discipline is the secret to long-term financial success. Don't be discouraged if you can only save a small amount. Sometimes, women tell me that they can't save an emergency fund because they could only put back a little each month. That's okay. Save what you can!

Once you have saved two-weeks' worth of your bills, you have enough in savings to cover minor, more common financial emergencies. But don't stop now! Once you have accomplished your initial goal, I want you to pat yourself on the back, and then do it again! Now, you have saved enough to cover one month of expenses. Keep going until eventually you have six months of nondiscretionary bills in savings, accumulated over time in realistic amounts.

By creating an emergency fund, you are accomplishing two different things. First, you are moving from being a spender to a saver. This is amazing, and it will help you get into the habit of putting money aside, whether it's for an emergency fund, your retirement, or the kids' college fund. Additionally, you now have enough money saved to cover most unexpected expenses. Even though you could easily need the entire six months of savings to cover losing your job, it's usually the smaller situations that get us financially off course. By having money in reserve and continuing to save more, you have started to turn the corner toward financial stability.

Megan: It will be challenging, but I know I can save enough money to pay two weeks of my bills. I'll just do it in five and ten dollar amounts that I can put back.

Jessica: It will be easy for me to start creating an emergency fund, because I just received a raise. I'll bet if I started now, I wouldn't even miss the amount I'm saving. If I wait, I'll find ways to spend it all every month.

Kim: I think rather than calling my plan an "emergency" fund, I'll call it a "fresh start." We really need to have at least six months in savings before I quit my job—maybe even more.

Sharon: I've had an emergency fund saved for years and let me tell you—it protected us many times from acquiring debt we didn't want.

Next Steps

Create a strategy for saving two weeks' worth of your bills. Once you have that much in a bank account, then try to do it again. Continue your two-week plan until you have saved several months of expenses. Jot down your notes on the following lines.

Chapter 4

Paying Off Debt

After making funny noises for months, the car engine blew, and replacing it just didn't make sense. They weren't huge, but the car payments took a bite out of her paycheck. Then, the refrigerator went out, and there were more payments. An unexpected root canal led to another monthly bill, and suddenly there wasn't enough money each month. Credit cards financed the balance, and she watched the debt grow bigger and bigger.

No one intends to incur debt. Many things can go wrong. Financial circumstances can change, unexpected, costly expenses can happen, and sometimes debt gradually grows over time. You didn't have one major event; however, a little overspending here and there, and all at once, you have a monster. What should you do?

First, own the situation, but don't beat yourself up. Yes, it matters why the debt happened, but guilt can paralyze you. You are where you are, so begin to take steps to improve your situation.

First, be sure that you are cash flow positive. We calculated cash flow in an earlier chapter, and if you have more bills each month than you have income, you need to make some adjustments. Begin by looking closely at the expenses you have. Find ways to spend less money. Or, alternatively, you may need to earn more income through a part-time job or a higher paying position.

If you want to spend less money, start with your discretionary purchases. Maybe it's time to cut the cord on cable television or those premium channels. Perhaps you need to stop eating out at work for lunch.

Go out less with your friends. Or better yet, I'll bet you're not the only one in your group who needs to watch expenses. Don't stop getting together—just do it at somebody's house, and bring your own bottle and snacks. For a more upscale evening, you could make a different craft cocktail each month, sharing the cost of the ingredients. You will all be amazed at how much you save. Each of you should start a "savings" page and write down the difference between what you would normally spend for a night out vs. your shared expenses. The positive reinforcement will keep you going.

Learn to cook at least on a basic level, and take a list to the store every time you go. Grocery bagging services will help you stay on track since you order your items in advance. I know you don't have a lot of time, but crock pots and instapots allow meal creation without great effort.

See if these lifestyle changes allow you to swing back to being cash flow positive. That's the first step to getting out of debt. If you're still under water, you may need to make larger changes around more affordable housing or an economical vehicle. You will also want to read the upcoming chapter on getting a better job.

If you're still not okay and you can't make ends meet, look into social assistance. Do you qualify for food stamps (now referred to as the SNAP program)? Low-income housing?

Medicaid or reduced insurance premiums under the Affordable Care Act? Is there a food pantry? Don't be ashamed to ask for help. Everyone has been in a jam. There's nothing wrong with using programs that are designed to keep you from financial disaster. If you like, vow to pay it forward once your circumstances improve. Just try to get your financial situation stable enough to stop increasing your card balances.

Once you have more income than expenses, then start paying off your debt. I have clients ask me whether they should pay off debt or save an emergency fund. I think you might want to do a little of both at the same time.

It can be difficult to decide which bill to pay off first. Most financial articles will tell you to begin with the highest interest rate. Certainly, if you have retail cards, they can have horribly high rates, and you want to pay those off as quickly as possible.

However, different people respond to debt in different ways. You may be most bothered by the number of places you owe money. If so, you might want to pay off smaller balances and lower your number of debts. On the other hand, you may be more concerned with the money you are losing in interest. If that's the case, then absolutely pay off the highest-rate credit cards first. However you do it, just start lowering your debt.

You will be successful if you create a strategy that you find useful and compelling, because this might be a long fight. Don't give up. If you could have all your debt paid off before you retired, you would sharply lower your monthly cash flow needs, because you wouldn't be losing any money paying for old purchases or interest. Once you have looked at your debt honestly, get a shovel and start digging your way out!

Megan: I have several small credit card bills that drive me crazy. I think I'll pay them off and then tackle the bigger debts.

Jessica: I have so many friends who are racking up credit card debt just trying to keep up with the latest fashion and decorating trends. I've paid off a card. I know how hard it is.

Kim: I'm worried about how I will fund a new business if I branch out on my own. I don't want to put all my business expenses on a credit card.

Sharon: I hate to see young people with debt, but I worry more about my friends. They are on a fixed income and don't have an easy way to earn additional money. Working a part-time job can be tough when you're older.

Next Steps

Make a list of all your debts and the minimum payments. Can you pay that amount? Do you have any additional funds in your budget? If so, choose one of your bills and pay more than the minimum—as much as you can. If you can't make the payments, look for ways to lower your spending. Jot down your ideas on the following lines.

Chapter 5

What is Financial Planning?

A woman came into my office for an initial meeting. She was currently working with an adviser and wasn't completely satisfied. Mostly, she wished the adviser would just answer her questions. She asked him things like, "Am I going to be okay to retire? Do I have enough money?" and "Do you have any ideas on how I could lower my tax liability?" Each time, the adviser would offer a vague promise of future advice, but none ever was offered.

THE PROFESSION of financial planning is young. Seeing clients as more than investment portfolios and insurance policies began in the 1960s by professionals who usually held licenses in both of these areas. They wanted to create a way to help people with their financial lives.

The field has evolved, changed, fought internally, and even taken on the Securities and Exchange Commission (SEC) and won, but at its heart, it's the same profession. Financial planning is holistic and concerned with helping people create financial goals and then organize and create the monetary resources required to meet them.

Financial planning helps you analyze what you make and what you own through cash flow and net worth statements. It also helps you develop ways of paying off debt and creating a savings plan.

Additionally, financial planning looks at your stock and bond portfolios as tools to help you meet your financial goals rather than exercises in taking as much risk as possible to earn the highest potential return. This context helps the client understand why the adviser's recommendations are made.

Insurance also takes a different perspective inside of financial planning. Even people who are highly suspicious of insurance salespeople and products understand the need to cover the catastrophic risks of unexpected death, disability, or illness. Because financial planning contextualizes insurance inside of cash flow, the insurance policy moves from a product to be sold to a tool to meet a need. A good financial planner can explain the reasons behind an insurance recommendation without just patting the purchasers on the head and telling them they need it.

Adequate retirement funding is critical for most people. Practically everyone is afraid of running out of money later in life. Financial planning takes a measured, thoughtful approach to determining your retirement need and creating strategies to fund it. True planning rarely uses rules of thumb and, instead, uses a cash flow analysis to help you decide how much money you will need to have available and what steps you should take to meet your goals.

Tax strategies are also an important part of financial planning. Remember that tax reduction and tax avoidance are great, while tax evasion can land you in jail! When you use the components and benefits of the tax code to lower your taxable income, you can save money. Additionally, tax planning comes into play on gifting strategies and inheritances.

Knowing the rules can be valuable. Most financial planners aren't tax preparers or CPAs, but they can offer valuable guidance and work in conjunction with your tax team.

Estate planning is also an important part of financial planning but is less likely to be covered in detail by a financial planner. This is because most financial planners, including me, aren't attorneys. However, your financial planner and your estate attorney should be partners.

In this book, we will explore financial planning as it relates to different parts of your life. In this section, we are reviewing some core basic concepts. Later, we will look at opening and running a business, juggling your parents and children (at the same time), surviving widowhood and divorce, thriving in the workplace, and creating ways to live your best life.

We will look at how your emotions impact your financial condition, but most of the book focuses on money, because money is always the center of your financial plan. Emotions, fears, and beliefs strongly impact your finances. However, at the end of the day, we are trying to be sure you have adequate financial resources to prosper.

Your financial plan begins, though, with setting your financial goals. Vague goals occur regularly in our day-in/day-out conversation, but they are difficult to achieve, because you're never really sure whether or not you are making progress. Instead, good financial goals should be concrete, know the associated costs, and have a way to calculate the timelines in which to achieve them.

So rather than saying, "I want to retire young," you would say, "I want to retire at sixty with a salary equal to 85% of my current income, because that's how much money I think I will need to live in the way I desire."

A financial planner cannot help you achieve a goal like

"retiring young." The planner can, however, help you calculate how to meet your specific targets.

The problem with "retiring young" is that you have no way to measure it. I know, measuring is scary. What if there isn't enough? Unfortunately, in financial planning, if you can't measure it, you probably can't achieve it. It's just the nature of the process.

Additionally, you will likely have multiple goals, and you will want to rank them in order of importance to you. All of us have limited financial resources. You may not have the ability to meet all of your financial goals, so decide what's most important to you, and work to achieve it.

Finally, creating a financial plan requires that you have your financial life organized. I know that some financial professionals will have you complete a questionnaire. What I have found, however, is that people often don't really understand the finer points of their financial lives.

As a result, your first step is to compile all the important financial documents. I've tried to make this process easier at the end of this chapter by giving you a list of potential items to compile. You won't need all of them, and you may have some documents I don't list here. However, it's a great place to start. It will help you understand the comprehensive nature of financial planning and will give you the tools to prioritize your goals.

∼

Megan: I don't really have any goals other than paying my bills. I would like to earn an associate's degree. I'd love to get a better job.

Jessica: I've never talked to anyone about my money. I wonder if I'm too young to meet with a planner.

Kim: Jessica, you aren't. I started working with a planner when I was about thirty. The earlier you can get started the better. I'm so glad Sam and I have worked with a comprehensive planner for years.

Sharon: I remember when we were juggling goals. There was only so much money, and it seemed like everyone wanted more than we had.

Next Steps

Before you continue with the further chapters in the book, take some time and put together the documents in the following list. Of course, if something doesn't apply to you, you won't have that document. But try to find everything that you can. Simply getting your arms around your financial life is a great first step!

Basic Documents

____ adoption papers
____ birth certificates
____ divorce documents
____ educational/training certificates
____ graduation certificates
____ passports

Financial Documents

____ advance directive
____ bank statements
____ brokerage statements and other investment accounts
____ business documents (if you own a business)
____ business plan (whether you have or hope to start one)
____ buy-sell agreements (if you own a business)
____ estate documents
____ investment documents
____ leases (car or home/apartment)
____ living will
____ pension statements
____ powers of attorney/durable powers
____ Social Security statements
____ succession plan (if you own a business)
____ trusts (family, literary, etc.)
____ wills

Insurance Documents

____ auto
____ disability
____ health (including Medicare, Medicaid, supplemental)
____ home (including flood, etc.)
____ life
____ long-term care

Latest Tax Return(s)

Cash-flow Document(s)

____ appliance/electronic equipment/etc. warranties
____ bank transactions (including ATM)
____ pay stubs
____ receipts for potentially deductible items
____ recurring bills (including credit card statements)

Net Worth Documents

____ current liabilities (loans, notes), interest rates, payoff
____ current value of major assets

Jot any notes on the following lines.

_____

_____

_____

_____

_____

Chapter 6

Retirement Planning Without Cat Food

When I answered the phone, on the other end was an older woman I knew well. She had attended a free dinner and financial seminar the night before, and she was nearly hysterical. The financial adviser informed everyone in the room that if they didn't have at least a million dollars in the bank, they would be eating cat food in retirement. Of course, they could solve their crisis if they purchased the product he was selling.

"Cat food?" I asked.

"Yes, cat food. He assured us that we couldn't trust Social Security or any pension we had earned. He said we would be eating cat food if we didn't take the resources we had and give them to him to invest."

I told her that I would be happy to help her evaluate her retirement resources. And then I assured her that his statements were designed to scare her and everyone else in the room. A blanket statement like the one he made was highly suspicious.

EVEN THOUGH I manage stock and bond portfolios, most of my clients' questions—especially from women—are not about the latest investment craze. In fact, they aren't about the stock market at all. What keeps these women up at night is the fear that they haven't saved enough for retirement. Most of them expect to be single, especially during their later years of life, and they know that the implications of any bad planning will fall on them. They want to know if they will be all right.

Trying to save enough money to fund the last thirty years of your life can be daunting. What makes this even scarier is the realization that you may be spending almost as many years in retirement as you spent working at a good job. How do you know how much to save, and how can you have confidence it's enough to avoid eating cat food?

From earlier chapters, you know I believe that an understanding of cash flow is critical for financial planning success. This is especially true when saving enough for retirement. You may have read about rules of thumb when it comes to how much you will spend during retirement, but I think they're risky. If you assume you'll spend 80% of your pre-retirement income and then you only spend 70%, your assumptions worked well. But what if you spend 90%? And exactly why is 80% such a good estimate?

I feel much more comfortable if you look at your current spending as a place to begin. Then, analyze those expenses to see which you would anticipate retaining during retirement. Yes, you likely will have paid your primary mortgage, but do you have the goal of a second home somewhere warm? If so, you could have a mortgage during your later years. If you enjoy sitting by the lake, that's great, but if you plan to see the world, that's more expensive.

Additionally, people tend to forget that during a thirty-year time horizon, they will purchase at least two or three vehicles. Regularly, clients tell me with a straight face that they don't plan to buy a vehicle, as they purchased one right before retirement. I ask them if they are going to drive it for twenty or thirty years, and when they laugh, we budget in the cost of the cars.

Of course, the real killer can be the cost of healthcare and late-in-life housing and nursing expenses. We will explore the cost of long-term care in a different chapter, but for now, just realize that aging is expensive.

Once you have a sense of what you will need each month during retirement, you should probably contact a CERTI-FIED FINANCIAL PLANNER™ practitioner to help with the compounding calculations. The process, although not actually difficult, is complex. Basically, you need to take the following questions into account:

• How many years will you be in retirement? Although no one knows their date of death, it's safe to assume that you may have significant longevity, living to ninety-five or one hundred.

• When do you want to retire? The longer you postpone retirement, the less money you will need.

• What will inflation do to your monthly need? The long-term rate for inflation is about 3%, so if you are still many years from retirement, your actual expenses will be significantly higher than they are today. In fact, every twenty-four years the cost of an item doubles at 3% inflation.

• What kind of investment assets do you want to hold? You can offset the impact of inflation by choosing a risk-appro-priate investment portfolio that, hopefully, lowers your need through market growth. Remember that the more conservative you want to remain, the more likely you are to have lower returns. Before you decide on a portfolio allocation, look at the anticipated return rate to determine whether or not it is sufficient to meet your needs.

• Do you have any pensions or benefits that will provide monthly income? Are they inflation adjusted? Many of the company pensions that still exist do not have an inflation component; however, Social Security does. I'm often asked if I think Social Security will still be there when people need it. I don't know if I'm an optimist or a cynic, but I believe that at the end of the day, no session of Congress wants to be the group to take away Social Security. Yes, the funding of the benefit needs attention, but that's possible in several ways. Obviously, if you can plan your retirement savings without needing Social Security, that's awesome. It's also quite unrealistic for many people.

• With the answers to these questions, are you on track to adequately fund your retirement? A CFP® pro can help you with these calculations. If you have enough money, congratulations! You're on track! If not, you can create a plan to correct your course.

Remember that the earlier you can start saving for retirement, the easier the process is. However, if you are getting a late start, don't despair. Just tackle it like your emergency fund. A little at a time is better than nothing. And remember that if sixty really is the new forty, like all the magazines tell us, it wouldn't be the end of the world if you worked a few extra years. This delaying of retirement is the easiest solution for funding a deficit, as you have additional time to save, and you don't begin to use your retirement resources as early.

For most people, the fear of not knowing how much money they need to save is worse than discovering they need to save a bit more. Although financial success involves many variables, if you take positive steps now, you won't need to be fighting kitty for the kibble. And you can laugh at the next person who tries to scare you with that sales pitch.

Megan: I like these ideas, but I want to focus on more immediate issues right now.

Jessica: I have no idea how much money I will need in retirement. I know I need to save as much as I can now, because time can really help compound the growth.

Kim: We should have paid off the house well before retirement. Also, if I love what I do for a living, I'm not sure I would want to retire fully at sixty-five or even seventy.

Sharon: I want to encourage my daughter to check her retirement progress. I think I remember that she is using the 80% rule of thumb, and I want her to track her cash flow instead.

Next Steps

Review your budget for expenses that will go up or down during retirement. Then, before you use an online calculator or contact a financial planner, locate your Social Security and pension statements, along with investment account documents. Finally, review your risk tolerance so you know your anticipated and historic rate of returns along with deciding an appropriate inflation rate. Jot your notes on the following lines.

Chapter 7

Calculating Life Insurance Need

I worried when a husband and wife came into my office, and the husband told me that he didn't need to purchase any life insurance. His wife was going to have more than enough money through his investment accounts and half his Social Security benefit. He went on to explain to me how life insurance is a rip off, and he wasn't going to be conned. His wife just sat there and looked at me. Shortly after the husband explained to me what a great job he had done, he left to go to the restroom. As soon as he left the room, the wife looked at me and said, "Talk some sense into him. I can't."

I UNDERSTAND why people can be skeptical of insurance recommendations. Stereotypes of fast-talking salespeople who hawk the latest product permeate our popular culture. Even worse, this stereotype sometimes mimics real events when agents can seem more interested in earning sales-based prizes rather than choosing the policy that is best for you.

However, a few bad actors have nothing to do with whether or not you need life insurance. Ignoring them, how do you know if you or your partner need to purchase insurance? Just like retirement savings, it isn't a rule of thumb. It's a math equation, and you already have the data.

Once more, we're going to look at your monthly spending. What would happen to you or your partner if one of your salaries went away? Can you survive financially? Here are a few questions to ask yourself.

• What final expenses need to be paid quickly?

• Would you be able to pay your bills on just one income along with any Social Security benefits paid to the minor children? If not, how much is your shortfall?

• Do you have children who will be attending college? Do you have the desire and resources to pay for this? What other expenses are associated with them? If something happens to one of you or you're single, their guardians may have costs like childcare that you don't have to pay today.

• Once you are no longer receiving Social Security benefits for your children, and they are out of the house, can you live on your own salary?

• Can you fund an adequate retirement plan? Remember by that point, in addition to your personal savings, you will have a Social Security benefit, possibly a pension from your deceased spouse, and access to his or her retirement savings.

If your answer is "no" for any of these periods of time, then you or your partner need to carry life insurance. To calculate the amount, take the shortfall and adjust it for inflation and, perhaps, modest investment growth using a compounding calculator. A financial planner can help you with this. The sum of the need for each of these time periods gives you the amount of insurance your partner should carry. You can offset this need by any amount of insurance that has already been purchased.

Additionally, I recommend that both partners run these calculations. In a relationship, one person usually earns more money than the other, sometimes by a significant amount. You may need your partner to carry insurance, while he or she may not need you to carry any. If you both run the numbers, you won't get an unpleasant surprise.

Once you know how much insurance you need, decide between term and whole life. Is there a point in time where you no longer have a deficit? For example, you might need money to pay for your children's college and to supplement your income until you are eligible for retirement. Then, by the time you are in retirement, you will have sufficient resources again. This suggests that, assuming no other influencing factors, your partner could purchase a term policy that lasts until you are ready for retirement. When a financial need is ongoing or exists longer than the length of the term, whole life might make more sense.

Life insurance can have many distinctive characteristics. Coverage can be permanent or temporary. Some policies tie to market returns, while others maintain a steady value. One type allows you to adjust the face value and premium payments. It can get complicated. If you want more information, I discussed the different kinds of life insurance in more detail in my first book, *52 Weeks to Prosperity*. Be certain that you understand the strengths and weaknesses of any policy you select.

Insurance salespeople often recommend purchasing whole life and using income multiples or estimates when calculating how much insurance to purchase. However, I believe a cash flow analysis will give you a closer estimate of your actual need. Of course, you can always buy additional coverage. If you and your partner choose to purchase a large policy that allows the survivor to live an easy life or not work at all, that might be a great idea. I just want the decision to be yours, not the insurance agent's.

Megan: What would happen to Charlotte if I were out of the picture? Buying adequate life insurance needs to be a priority.

Jessica: I'm not married, and I don't have any children. I have a $50,000 life insurance policy from work, and right now my mom is the beneficiary. I don't think I need anything else.

Kim: Wow, every time I turn around, I need to anticipate another expense if I leave my job. I wonder if my employer allows me to keep my policy if I leave and how much it would cost.

Sharon: I'm so glad that my kids are financially stable. I don't have a large insurance need—just enough to bury me. I've had that policy paid up in full for years.

Next Steps

In this chapter you will use anticipated costs and any existing life insurance policies to provide the data to do an insurance analysis using cash flow. You may find a calculator difficult to locate, so you will likely want to contact a financial planner. Just ask them how they determine insurance

need before you meet with them. Jot any notes on the
following lines.

Chapter 8

How to Read a Portfolio Statement

After reading an article about investment "churning," an older client wanted to see how many times her former broker placed a trade each month. She had never paid attention to her monthly statements other than looking at the balance on the top of the first page. She was amazed at the statement's length, and she didn't understand most of it. She asked me to help her unravel the document.

READING financial documents can be daunting. The brokerage statement you receive periodically is no exception. Many people don't even know what they are looking at after the first page. In this chapter, I want to help you look past that and review the major sections.

The order might be different, and there might be sections on your statement in addition to the ones I describe here. If that's the case, have your financial planner assist you in understanding any additional data.

Date Range

The top of your statement should have the period of time covered by the statement. They might be monthly, quarterly, or annual. Some firms send monthly statements, but many only send quarterly unless there has been a purchase, sale, or other type of transaction during the month. If you save them, always doublecheck that you are looking at the most current document for up-to-date performance and transaction history.

Gains/Losses of the Period

Near the date range, you should see data indicating whether or not your account made money during the period of time you are reviewing. This section typically includes a beginning balance, an ending balance, money you deposited, money you withdrew, and any fees you were charged. A second column may include the portfolio performance on a year-to-date (YTD) basis, as well.

List of Holdings

The next section of your statement is likely a list of your investment holdings. This list will include a description of each holding, along with how much money is in that investment. Additionally, any cash or money market you hold will be included. The total of this section will be the same number as your portfolio's current value.

Sometimes, the investment's description will include a series of capitalized letters after the name of the holding. These letters create the "symbol" for your investment—a shortcut method of identifying precisely what you own. Using the symbol, you can research investment characteristics and fees. If your investment statement doesn't provide symbols, ask your financial adviser for a list of them.

Some investments don't have symbols. If your adviser tells you this is the case, ask him or her to send you the portion of the prospectus that provides the fund descriptions, including any fees. The prospectus is a technical, lengthy description of an investment. It's a tough read, but it contains valuable information.

Gains and Losses of Each Position

The gains or losses of each position might be included in the previous section, but more likely they are provided in a different part of the statement. This section will also show the date you purchased the investment. Remember that the gain or loss described here shows the performance over the length of time you owned the investment. It's likely you show a gain or loss on this page that does not agree with the performance during the time period of the statement.

Your overall gain or loss is particularly important for two reasons. First, it helps you track how well your investments have performed. Additionally, if the investment account is taxable, the gain/loss statement shows tax implications if the positions are sold. You may owe capital gains or be able to deduct capital losses.

Dividends and Interest

A separate section in your statement should list any dividends and interest you earned during the time period of the statement. Remember that dividends are usually paid by stocks or stock funds, while interest is paid by bonds, bond funds, money market, and other types of fixed income. This section is relatively easy to understand, and each event is listed separately.

Activity

The activity section of your brokerage statement is, by far, the most potentially confusing. To understand what you are reviewing, let's start with background information. The dividends and interest paid by your investments that we discussed above are paid to your account in cash. However, investment accounts aren't allowed to hold literal "cash."

Instead, each night the cash sweeps into a money market account. From an activity perspective, this will show as a negative balance, line-item cash transaction and an offsetting positive balance, line-item money market transaction. For example, if you have a stock that pays a $100 dividend, you may see offsetting activity of -$100 cash; +$100 money market.

To make it worse, if multiple transactions occur on the same day of the month, you may see individual negative balance line items with just one positive balance line item, where all of the transactions sweep into money market on the same line.

The activity section will also show you any purchases, sales, dividends paid, interest paid, distributions you took from the account, and fees deducted from the account.

If you are concerned with this part of your statement, you might want to schedule a meeting with your financial planner and let him or her explain it to you line by line. Once you understand exactly how your custodian reports the activity, it's much easier to review.

Disclaimers

Your brokerage statement usually ends with pages and pages of disclaimers. I think it's always smart to review these at least once. It's a lot of legal language, and usually there isn't anything here that is extremely problematic or adjustable. Perhaps the most disturbing sentence you may find, buried in the middle of this document, is the line "Your interests might not be our interests," or words to those effect.

This disclaimer is why it's so important to talk to your financial adviser about whether he or she is acting in your best interest. The custodian really is just a broker of trades, but there are times when brokerage firms tip their hand on how their representatives treat their clients. We'll talk more about this in a separate chapter.

Understanding how to read your brokerage statement makes it less intimidating. By taking time to review it, along with asking questions about anything you don't understand, you will soon find that it's a document that gives you a wealth of information about your portfolio performance.

Megan: I don't have any investments, but my mom does. She got half of my dad's retirement account when they divorced. I'm going to show her this chapter.

Jessica: I have such a hard time reading my 401(k) statement. Maybe now I can figure out how my investments are performing rather than seeing if the total balance is higher or lower.

Kim: I've used a financial planner for years, but I've never really paid attention to the details in my statement. I'll give her a call for a meeting and ask her to help me break it apart.

Sharon: I always worry about women who just let their husbands take care of the investment accounts. My George always took the time to explain the holdings to me, and now I can read my statement pretty easily.

Next Steps

Review several brokerage statements to help determine trading patterns, expenses, holdings, and returns over different periods of time. Then, make it a practice to look at your statement each time it is available. Jot some notes on the following lines.

_____

_____

_____

_____

_____

Chapter 9

Basics of Investing

Investing is confusing to many people, regardless of gender. I have found that both men and women, when they are in a safe environment, are willing to admit they have investment questions. However, they often approach their concern differently to me. Men seem uncomfortable and concerned with their lack of understanding. However, some women almost seem to embrace their confusion. They tell me that investing "just isn't their thing." But the data suggests otherwise.

DID you know that research shows that women are often better investors than men? Really. How can that be true when women don't often sit around talking about the latest stock or how our genius cryptocurrency decision led to a 400% rate of return? In fact, if we do discuss investing, unfortunately many of us talk about not being very good at it.

If guys talk about their stellar stock-picking prowess more often than women, why are we better at it? I think investing for many women is a means to an end, a place where we are forced to participate.

We know we can't save enough to pay for our children's

education by putting money in a bank, so we contribute to a 529 plan or a Coverdell Education Savings account. We're terrified of running out of money in our old age, so we fund retirement accounts. We know we will probably be by ourselves at some point in our lives, and we save extra just because we want to be comfortable.

In short, we put investing into the context of financial planning. This perspective is useful for several reasons. First, since we invest as a way to meet a goal, we know how many years we have until we need the money. One of the key components of creating a risk tolerance level that we can live with AND lets us meet our goals is knowing how long the money can be invested. If we need money almost immediately, it probably should be invested in something with little or no market risk. But if we have more time, we may be able to take more risk.

People are funny in their reaction to stock market volatility. Nearly always, they will acknowledge that they know the market goes up and the market goes down. As part of the disclaimers that financial advisers provide to their clients, they remind us that investing is risky, and we can lose money. A few people might not know that, but most people understand that the market is volatile. I think a better disclaimer would be, "Investing is risky, and you might lose money at exactly the wrong time. As a result, choose an appropriate risk tolerance level."

Because women tend to invest for goals, they are likely to understand that disclaimer. However, when people invest for pure return, all day, every day, then any market decline is scary. Investments can be traded at exactly the wrong moment, and losses are locked in place. Just that reason alone explains to me why women have a slight investing edge.

Additionally, many women readily admit that they are not

investing geniuses. This recognition helps avoid an interest in high-flying investments, but it concerns me, as well. As a result, I want to take the rest of the chapter to explain the basics of the stock market. You should feel confident that your investment portfolio was made from a good series of decisions.

First, portfolios are invested following an asset allocation, or a blend of investments like stocks and bonds, that has been chosen as a result of the goal for the money. The risk of the portfolio depends on the types of asset classes you choose.

The most common asset class is equities. For most of us, equity is basically a high-dollar word meaning stock. Many of us don't select single equities; we invest in funds (usually mutual funds or exchange traded funds) of equities. When we buy a fund, we buy a collection of investments that have something in common. For example, a large-cap domestic equity fund is a collection of stocks made up of large American companies. Equity funds can be composed of many different things, including US large cap, mid cap, or small cap, developed or emerging foreign countries, or sectors of the US stock market like "technology" or "healthcare."

Equities provide a positive return through both price increase and dividends. Different kinds of stocks focus on these two goals differently, so you might invest in a fund that focuses on stock growth, you might select one that invests for regular dividend payments, or you might select a fund that focuses on both. Of course, sometimes stock prices go down, and the fund loses value. Less commonly, a company that is changing its focus might cut its dividend. This is particularly painful for older investors who often seek income more than growth.

The next major asset class is fixed income, usually in the form of bonds, although there are other kinds of fixed income. I know that bonds don't have the sexy reputation that stocks have, but I want you to spend a little time understanding fixed income. There are different risk levels, depending on whether you choose government treasuries, government agencies, corporate, or international bonds. Bonds also have different risk levels depending on their time horizon. Remember that when you buy a bond, you are making a loan to the entity issuing it. Shorter-term loans are generally less risky than longer-term ones because the entity has less time to make a financial mistake, leaving them unable to pay you.

Bond funds pay money two ways. First is through an actual increase in the value of the fund, indicating that the cost of the bond has gone up. More often, though, bond funds are purchased because they pay money through yield, commonly called interest. Remember that the riskier the bond, the more interest it will pay—in the same way that a poor credit score increases the interest you will pay on a loan. As a result, bonds that pay a high yield provide more income, but you are taking more risk to get that money.

Other common asset classes are "real estate," "commodities," and "cash or cash equivalents." They are pretty much exactly what they sound like. A word of caution here: diversification is nearly always your friend. One way that people were badly hurt in 2008 was through focusing too much on real estate. In that case, some of them were losing their literal homes along with their investment portfolios at the same time. Commodities like oil and gold can also be enticing, but be careful not to focus too many of your assets in narrow areas.

Cash, money markets, and their equivalents are very safe, and as a result earn a low rate of return. Remember when we talked about the impact of inflation on your retirement and insurance expenses? It's important to keep your investment portfolio earning an overall return higher than the inflation rate. That's why when your money is under your mattress (or even in just money market), you're likely losing a little bit of its value every single day.

If the mattress isn't a good option, then how do you choose the correct asset allocation? To make this decision effectively, it's important to understand the purpose of a risk tolerance level. Your risk tolerance is a way to determine both that you take a prudent and appropriate amount of risk in your portfolio and that your investments don't keep you up at night. Remember that your risk tolerance isn't static. It might change with life circumstances. Additionally, different financial goals could have different risk tolerance levels.

For instance, let's assume that you have a thirteen-year-old daughter, and you are saving for her college education. Additionally, you're about forty years old, and you plan to retire at the age of sixty-five. In your daughter's college fund, you are five years from the goal, and you will probably begin to lower the level of risk in those investments. However, with twenty-five years until retirement, there's no reason you couldn't be somewhat aggressive in that investment strategy.

I want you to complete your risk tolerance levels in conjunction with your goals. Always be certain that the tolerance you seek matches the way that your money is invested. If you have defined yourself as moderate, possibly seeking a 5%-6% inflation-adjusted rate of return, but your retirement savings calculation uses an 8% rate, then your retirement plan is doomed to failure. You can solve this situation several different ways, but what you shouldn't do is ignore it and hope that everything will be okay. You may not want to raise the risk level of your portfolio, but you could plan to work a few extra years or perhaps save a little more money. If you opt to increase your risk level, do it cautiously with the guidance of a financial planner.

In most economic environments, the stock market is the

engine of growth in your investment portfolio. The higher the risk tolerance you have, the more percent of equities (stock) you are likely to own. As reference, the long-term average rate of return for equities is 11%. Of course, with higher potential return comes a greater level of risk. We've all seen the stock market decline, sometimes significantly. Even in major downturns, broad sections of the market recover in less than five years, but specific sectors can take much longer, and individual companies can go under, never to be seen again. That's why diversifying within your equity ownership makes sense.

You also need to diversify outside of your equities into asset classes that respond much differently in a poor stock market environment. Perhaps the best diversifier is fixed income. As the stock market declines, the bond market, especially the US government bond market, usually responds well as investors fly to safety. However, bonds aren't without risks. A rising interest rate environment can create difficulties in the bond market. And corporate bonds can be subject to default if the company that issued them cannot pay their bills. However, bonds typically have less volatility and are usually held in higher percentages in more conservative portfolios.

If you make your own investment decisions, you will want to do significant research. Even if you work with a CERTI-FIED FINANCIAL PLANNER™ practitioner acting as your fiduciary, or in a way that puts your interests ahead of his or hers, take the time to understand your investments. It's much easier to choose an effective asset allocation and stay the course when you understand both your investment goals and why your different investments respond the way they do.

〜

Megan: I learned a little bit about money in high school, but not nearly enough to help me make investment decisions. I wish the schools would offer a more comprehensive curriculum.

Jessica: Originally, I chose a target date fund for my 401(k). As my account size increased, I made more specific decisions.

Kim: Our financial planner has spent many hours helping my partner and me understand our investments. I don't know a lot about the market, but I really think I understand the fundamentals.

Sharon: My husband never chased the latest fad, and he encouraged me to do the same. As a result, we lost money in every downturn, but we didn't have horrible losses. If a financial adviser made other recommendations, we just ignored him.

Next Steps

We talked about how to read investment statements in the last chapter. Using that information, look at your asset allocation —your blend of different asset classes—and talk to your financial planner about the risk level you are taking and what you should expect as realistic rates of return. Jot some notes on the following lines.

Chapter 10

Retirement Plans

Early in my career, I helped a woman complete a data ques-
tionnaire I had given her. Once finished, I planned to use that
data to create a financial plan. When we got to the section
where she provided information about her investment
accounts, she told me that she had an IRA at her workplace. I
asked her if perhaps she had meant a 401(k). She said no; she
was pretty sure her employer offered an IRA. I didn't tell her
that employers actually can't offer IRAs, so instead, I asked her
for a copy of her statement. When she mailed it to me, sure
enough, it was a 401(k).

ONCE YOU KNOW how much money you need to save for
retirement, then you must decide what kinds of retirement
accounts will help you reach your goals. However, the options
can be confusing, and often you may hear conflicting advice.
Let's take time to look at different kinds of plans and their
characteristics.

First, if you have a company retirement plan, you probably want to participate in it. Company retirement plans take
many forms, but some of the most common are 401(k) or

403(b). Each type of plan has distinguishing characteristics, and you need to understand them with the help of your Human Resources (HR) department. One of the most important considerations is whether or not your employer contributes to the plan or matches your deferrals.

The employer contribution or match is such an advantage for employees. If employers provide a contribution, this means that they put money in your account for you whether you make any contribution or not. If they match, that means if you put money in your account, the company will match your contribution up to a certain percent of your salary, often 3%.

This is awesome! It's free money. I know some financial celebrities have been critical of company retirement plans and have given the advice to fund individual retirement accounts instead. However, I don't know why you would turn down free money from your employer.

Of course, check with your own financial planner. Also, the plans may have limited investment options, and sometimes the fees associated with the available funds could be higher than I might like. But it's free money. Go ahead. Take it.

Consider funding your company plan with money in addition to the amount of their match. You know, "great" really is the enemy of "good." It's easy to participate in your company plan; the HR department and plan sponsor can explain any details to you, and you can defer considerable money into it. In fact, for many Americans, the amount they are allowed to defer into their plans exceeds the amount they can actually afford to lose out of their money paycheck. You can defer $22,500 in 2023 or $30,000 if you are age 50 or older. The ability to defer that much money into your account can really help your retirement savings.

If you work for a small employer, you are less likely to

have a 401(k) plan, and they are more likely to offer a SEP (Simplified Employee Pension) plan or a SIMPLE (Savings Incentive Match Plan for Employees). If your employer offers a SEP, you don't make contributions to that plan, but your employer does. Although they don't have to do it annually, they do make substantial and recurring contributions. If your employer offers the SIMPLE, you can defer up to $15,500 a year in 2023 with an additional $3,500 if you are over fifty. In addition to this, your employer may offer a nonelective contribution or a match. Like a 401(k), you should take advantage of the match to receive the free money! If you are a small business owner, we're going to talk about these plans from your perspective later in the book.

Unfortunately, you may not work for an employer that offers a retirement plan, or if you work two or three part-time jobs, you may not have access to any of the plans that exist. If that's the case, then saving for your retirement is up to you. Fortunately, the IRS has created two different savings vehicles to assist you with this: the traditional Individual Retirement Account (IRA) and the Roth Individual Retirement Account.

Both traditional IRAs and Roth IRAs allow the same levels of deferral--$6,500. If you are fifty or over, you can contribute an additional $1,000. The difference between the traditional IRA and the Roth is the tax treatment. For most participants, traditional IRAs are funded in pre-tax dollars with ordinary income tax due on distributions. Roth IRAs are funded in after-tax dollars, but if you follow the rules, you never pay income tax on the growth.

You may not know that everyone can, in fact, fund a traditional IRA. The only catch is that sometimes you can deduct that contribution, and sometimes you can't, depending on your income level and retirement plan participation. Most people think about contributing to an IRA and taking a tax deduction for the amount of the contribution. If you don't have a retirement plan offered by your employer or there's a plan, but no money went into the account on your behalf, you can most likely deduct your IRA. If you participate in a retirement plan or if you are married, and your spouse participates in a company plan, then there is an adjusted gross income (AGI) phaseout for deductibility.

If you can't deduct your traditional IRA contribution, why would you still fund it? One of the most common reasons is the ability to make portfolio changes without triggering capital gains tax. Specifically, once any IRA is funded, then no additional tax is owed until you take a distribution from the account. If you sell one security and purchase another one inside your IRA, there are no tax consequences. Instead, you have a basis (after tax) amount of contribution with ordinary income tax due only on the amount of the gain.

Before you decide to go down this road, however, there is one important caveat that I need to mention. If your income level is such that you are in the bottom two tax brackets, you don't pay capital gains tax anyway. I find that many clients of moderate means may not have capital gains avoidance as an issue. However, if you are in a higher bracket, capital gains tax is a consideration, and you can avoid that liability in the traditional, nondeductible IRA.

Funding a nondeductible IRA has a much greater advantage, as well—the ability to do a Roth conversion. In a Roth conversion, traditional IRA money is moved to a Roth IRA, and any taxes are paid. The net funds are now in the Roth IRA and subject to the Roth rules.

To understand why the conversion strategy is popular, let's look at Roth IRAs for a minute. You fund the account in after-tax dollars, and as a result, you don't get the tax deduction today. However, if you leave the account open for five years, and you are 59½, all the growth of the account can be distributed income tax free. In today's tax environment, I think this may make a lot of sense. Let me tell you why.

I believe it's likely that the next income tax movement will be up, not down. In other words, I believe that in the future, people will be paying more money in taxes rather than less. The need to pay our national bills and reduce the deficit suggests a tax increase will happen sometime in the not-so-distant future.

Additionally, remember that the individual tax benefits in the Tax Cuts and Jobs Act go away after 2025. The corporate tax cuts were permanent, but ours weren't. Now, I'm rarely an alarmist, but I do think that people planning for their retirement need to think about what tax bracket they anticipate during that period of time. Especially if you have been a good saver, have a pension, or additional resources, your retirement assets could be substantial. You could find yourself in a tax bracket as high as your current rate (or higher), assuming even a modest increase to taxes.

This is one of the best reasons to fund a Roth IRA directly or through the "back door" Roth conversion. The tax-free growth may be important in the future. Remember that Roth IRAs have an adjusted gross income (AGI) phaseout. If you earn income higher than the phaseout level, you can't fund a Roth at all, whether or not you participate in your company's plan.

Fortunately, however, the Roth conversions we were discussing earlier don't have that limitation. You can convert funds from a traditional IRA to a Roth with no income constraints. As a result, if you earn too much money to deduct a Roth or a traditional IRA, you may want to fund a nondeductible IRA with the idea of completing a Roth conversion.

Remember that you will pay income tax on the amount converted.

Think through your Roth conversion before you complete it. Recent legislation no longer allows you to change it back to a traditional IRA through a recharacterization. However, if you proceed carefully, that strategy shouldn't be necessary. Sometimes, Roth conversions aren't effective, so check with your planner and CPA first.

You have many options for funding your retirement in tax favored ways. Take time to look at your available options, talk to your financial planner, and choose what will provide you with adequate funding. You want your retirement years to be financially easy, not stressful.

Megan: The list of what I need to do keeps growing. I will fund an IRA as soon as I can.

Jessica: I also have a Roth component to my 401(k). I'm paying taxes on my deferrals now, so I won't have to pay them later.

Kim: We have a good diversification of pre-tax accounts, after-tax accounts, and Roths. I like the idea of having different tax treatments for our money, since I don't really know what I think is happening to the tax code in the future.

Sharon: I've been completing a partial Roth conversion each year for a while now. I think taxes are going up, too. Even if they don't, I like the stability of knowing how much money I have without worrying about my liability.

Next Steps

Look at each investment account you have, and decide whether it is currently taxable, tax deferred, or potentially tax free. If you don't understand the details of any of the accounts, talk to your financial planner, CPA, or HR department at work. Then, check your income level to see if you have any funding options you were overlooking. Jot some notes on the following lines.

Chapter 11

What to Do When There's No Money

The money had been tight but adequate before she got cancer. Thank God, she had beaten it, but the medical bills were overwhelming. She hated to admit she needed financial assistance, and worse than that, she didn't know where to look.

It's hard to admit you need help. When you are in a true financial crisis, the situation is overwhelming. Maybe you made some mistakes or life just dealt cards that were too difficult. In any case, don't be ashamed to reach out and take advantage of government resources.

A good place to start is your state's Department of Human Services. Their website will summarize available programs, as they can differ between states. You can also search for aid that matches your individual circumstances.

Some programs are also commonly available nationally. One of these is healthcare through either Medicaid or the Affordable Care Act (ACA), commonly called Obamacare. Medicaid is available for low-income individuals or families. If you qualify, the healthcare is either free or low cost. ACA premiums are based on your income and may be more affordable to you if you earn too much money to qualify for Medicaid.

Food assistance is available through the Supplemental Nutrition Assistance Program (SNAP). Also called "food stamps," SNAP provides a benefit card that can be used to purchase groceries. Nursing mothers and young children can also receive food and vouchers through the Women, Infants, and Children (WIC) program.

Cash assistance is available through the Temporary Assistance for Needy Families (TANF) program. If you are working to improve your situation and need some temporary financial assistance, TANF can provide supplemental income.

Another program is specifically designed for young children. Head Start provides numerous benefits including early childhood education for low-income children between birth and age five. Kids may also qualify for free meal programs at school. Sometimes, the benefits include breakfast and weekend supplements in addition to lunch.

If you want to buy a home but don't qualify for a conventional mortgage, look into the HOPE I program. "Homeownership and Opportunity for People Everywhere" provides funds for nonprofit organizations. These funds are used to create home ownership programs that allow low-income individuals and families to purchase public housing units.

Additionally, FHA loans can allow home ownership. You can qualify with a weaker credit score and less money for a down payment. Although these characteristics may allow you to purchase property, work with a financial planner to be sure you can afford the payments along with your other financial obligations.

If renting an apartment proves to be a better option, you may be able to receive rent assistance through the Housing Choice Voucher Program. Further, the Low-Income Home

Energy Assistance Program (LIHEAP) can assist with energy bills.

Finally, when you file your taxes, don't forget the Earned Income Tax Credit (EITC). Tax credits are a dollar-for-dollar reduction in tax liability, and the EITC is available to low-income tax filers.

Many government services exist to help you get back on your feet, and more are created regularly. Look into the details of these and other programs. Remember to review maximum income levels and other limitations. There's no shame in using a safety net. You can pay it forward when things get better.

Megan: I'm going to look into a few of these programs. I didn't know I could get help paying my electric bill.

Jessica: I have some friends who don't earn enough money to qualify for ACA, but our state doesn't offer expanded Medicaid. In spite of all the progress, they still can't purchase healthcare.

Kim: Social programs are so important to our society. We want to take care of our most fragile community members.

Sharon: Older people on limited incomes often need these services too. I have several friends who live in public housing.

Next Steps

If you're struggling financially, look into potential benefits and what you would need to qualify. Jot some notes on the following lines.

Chapter 12

Choosing a Financial Professional

A young woman was just getting started in her professional career. She was trying to pay off some debt and begin to save for her retirement. Her father had died several years before, and she wanted to be sure her mom would be okay. She told me that her financial adviser had recommended that she purchase a whole life insurance policy. Even though it was expensive, he had promised her that this was the only way to guarantee her mother would be financially secure. After I had asked a few more questions, I realized the woman was really only concerned what would happen to her mom over the next ten years or so, as she anticipated being in a better financial position to help in the future. I explained the difference between whole and term life and showed her how she could take care of her mother over the next decade for considerably less money.

As you can see in this first section, your financial life is extremely complicated. Collaborating with a good financial adviser can make your life much easier, but finding the right person can be difficult. How do you know who to trust?

I think the single most important characteristic of your

financial adviser is his or her willingness to serve as a fiduciary. A financial fiduciary standard is a legal obligation for an adviser to act in a client's best interest. The rule doesn't prevent the adviser from being paid, but it does suggest that fees should be fair. Additionally, product decisions, like investments or insurance, should be made with the client's best interest as the focus rather than the compensation received by the adviser. The adviser-as-fiduciary landscape has been changing regularly for the past few years, so let me review a few of the issues with you.

Wouldn't you think that the person you entrusted with your life savings, your hard-earned money, would do his or her best to act in your best interest? Sure, you would! But guess what? That's not the law. In fact, as of this writing many financial advisers have no fiduciary obligation to you. To make it even worse, recent legislation has incorporated words like "best interest" into a degree of care that still falls short of the legal standard of fiduciary. Nevertheless, it's important to have your financial adviser agree to hold a fiduciary duty. If he or she dances around your question and refuses to commit to a fiduciary level of care for you (in writing), you might want to consider a different adviser.

Next, do you need a financial planner? Remember that a financial planner contextualizes your financial decisions inside your financial needs and life. In this role, financial planners will assist you with cash flow issues, saving an emergency fund, and paying off debt. They help you manage risk by explaining the characteristics of different kinds of insurance products and provide you with any appropriate alternatives within these products.

Financial planners assist you with your investment portfolio, helping you select a risk tolerance level and appropriate asset allocation to help you meet your financial goals. Financial planners can calculate how much money you need to save for retirement and explain the characteristics of your company retirement plan along with other retirement savings vehicle options, like IRAs.

Planners also look at your tax situation and try to find ways to reduce your tax liability, and they look at your estate issues. If they aren't an attorney, they should encourage you to seek advice from one as you create your plan.

Additionally, planners provide guidance with other types of financial concerns, including paying for college and buying or leasing a vehicle. If you're trying to organize elements of your financial life, a financial planner can help.

One area where financial services can be very confusing is in the sea of acronyms. Advisers may have a laundry list after their name of various sundry designations. Be sure to ask the focus and requirements of each of them. Some are rigorous, and some aren't, and it's important you see the difference.

It's my opinion that the CERTIFIED FINANCIAL PLANNER™ practitioner standard is the designation to seek when you want to work with a financial planner. If you read the disclaimers at the beginning of this book, you will see that any time I refer to a "financial planner" in this book I mean a CERTIFIED FINANCIAL PLANNER™ practitioner.

The CFP® pro designation has a six-hour closed book exam following a full year of coursework. There are twenty hours of Continuing Education that must be earned every two years, including an Ethics course. CFP® pros have at least a bachelor's degree (in any program of study) and three or more years of experience in financial planning. They also are required to embrace that all-important fiduciary duty. It really is the gold standard for financial planners.

Of course, if you don't want financial planning, you may want your adviser to have a different designation. My belief is that you should work with the best person you can find and whose model is appropriate to your needs. It's reasonable to expect them to have additional education beyond their licenses. After all, you're trusting them with a lot.

After reviewing their willingness to be a fiduciary and what services they offer, I think there are a few additional issues. Even though designations and training are very important, your adviser should also treat you with respect. Too many times, women feel as though their financial advisers pat them on their heads and tell them not to worry about anything. Now, I'm not suggesting you take a course in finance, but I am also very distrusting of advisers who can't explain how they reach their recommendations. Maybe you really do need a million dollars of life insurance, but don't just believe agents who suggest that amount. Ask them how they came to their conclusion.

I think selecting a financial adviser can be difficult for women. You should expect them to treat you as intelligent, talk to you, not just your husband if you're married, and take an active role in your finances. I worry that much of the current focus on marketing towards women is based on the demographic knowledge held by the financial firms. Wealth is passing to women as male baby boomers are dying and as more women are choosing to stay single. But you are more than a marketing campaign, and your assets will have to sustain you through your life, not just be additional assets under management to your adviser. Good planners and advisers know this, so it's up to you to find them.

Megan: It's so hard to get good financial advice when you don't have a lot of money, or any money. I need help.

Jessica: The only financial adviser I know is the guy who comes to explain our company's 401(k) plan. He talks awfully fast, though. I wouldn't want to use him outside of the office.

Kim: We have a fabulous female financial planner. She has done a great job creating a holistic plan for us. And she's been guiding us through my idea of a new business, as well.

Sharon: I have used a financial planner for years, but I also make many of my own decisions. I don't know if it's the right thing for most people because I had the time to do it. Still, I always appreciated having someone who could answer my questions.

Next Steps

If you are looking for a financial professional, take some time to interview people before you make a choice. Several consumer-facing organizations offer questionnaires you can download to help you make your decisions. Use the following lines to write down your notes.

Starting a Business

Mary Kies: First Woman to Receive a Patent in the United States

THE PATENT ACT of 1790 allowed both men and women to protect inventions with a patent. However, at this time a woman couldn't own property independent of her husband. As a result, women typically didn't apply for patents. However, Mary Kies had developed a process for weaving straw with thread or silk and used her creation when building beautiful hats. On May 15, 1809, Mary received a patent for her process.

Part of the reason for her success was the fashion crisis occurring in the United States. England and France were engaged in the Napoleonic Wars, and England did not want the United States to stay neutral. In response to the pressure, President Thomas Jefferson prohibited the importing of English goods, and American fashion began to suffer.

American women were hungry for new fashion, and Mary's woven hats were a huge success. When President Madison presented her with her patent, First Lady Dolly Madison thanked her for her accomplishment.

Soon, due to Mary's technique and other improvements to hat making, a cottage industry of hat making spread across

New England, giving women the ability to earn money and wear the latest styles.

Although her hats were popular for a decade, she found it difficult to make her business a financial success. Additionally, fashion changed, and Mary's hats fell out of style. After the death of her husband, she moved to Brooklyn to live with her son. She was buried in a pauper's grave at the age of 83.

Chapter 13

Starting a Business

When I decided I wanted to open my own business, the people I knew tended to fall into three categories. The first group, by far the largest percent, thought I had lost my mind. They loved me, but they didn't understand why I would leave a good job to pursue both a new venture and a new profession. The level of risk made them crazy. The second group, which were mostly acquaintances, thought it was great I had my own business. They wanted their own businesses, too, so they could kiss their supervisors goodbye and go to work when they wanted to. The third group knew I was in for a tough time but also thought I could do it. They offered support and useful advice. If you are thinking about starting your own business, as much as you can, surround yourself with people who believe in you.

So you want to start a business? Congratulations! Being an entrepreneur can be very rewarding. Still, owning a business can be challenging. Twenty percent of all small businesses fail in the first year, and fifty percent have failed by the fifth year. You want to do everything you can to stack the odds in your favor, so before we look at issues like business plans, entities,

222222222222222

retirement plans, and other topics, I want to ask you some important questions to help you succeed.

First, why do you want your own business? There are many great answers. However, all of them should involve having a passion for what you will be doing. You are going to spend so much time and money getting this off the ground that if you don't love your business, it will be very difficult to make it work.

Now of course, some businesses require more work than others, but all of them will take hours and hours of time. If you chose a venture on a whim or because the earning potential is high and you know a person in the field who made a lot of money doing it, please think some more, and do additional research.

Do you want your own business because you think you will get additional vacation time? When I opened my financial firm, I was surprised how many people told me that it must be nice to get to take off any time I chose. I told them it was—I got to work any sixty hours a week that I wanted! I wasn't kidding. Running your own business will take an incredible amount of time, and it will be the hardest work you ever did. You will have days that you feel amazingly successful and days when you know you have made the biggest mistake of your life. If you want to own your own business because you're sure you want to work less, you probably should abandon the idea before you lose a lot of money.

As you read this, it almost sounds like I'm trying to talk you out of starting your own business. No, I'm not; I just don't want you to go into the venture thinking it's something it isn't. Starting a business, even a part-time one, has many values. For example, if you're careful, it can be a great way to earn money to meet financial goals. Additionally, it's one of the most rewarding tasks you can undertake.

We will be talking about creating a business plan in a different chapter, but as you are considering opening a business, you should start by looking at your goals. To that end, are you trying to create a career or earn some additional money? Different kinds of ventures will lead to different outcomes. Remember that the more complex your business, the more you will have to pay in start-up costs and overhead. On the other hand, some business activities can be run part time, leaving you free to have a primary career or take care of things around the home. You might also want to work a few hours a week during retirement. In fact, this can be a good way to stretch your retirement resources.

However, if owning a business is part of your retirement plan, you need to be careful. I've seen advertisements for part-time work that offer insanely high potential compensation. I'm sure once in a while this happens, but it's not likely. You need to have a realistic expectation of the money you will earn. "Get rich quick" plans usually work best for the person who tries to convince you to pursue the venture. And remember the start-up costs and potential failure rate before you spend precious retirement resources on a system that could easily fail.

So do your research, answer the questions, and then if it looks good, go for it! Just know what you want out of your business before you open it.

Megan: I really wish those online ads about how to make a six-figure salary were true. I always thought they sounded fishy.

Jessica: I have so many friends who are selling different products. I'm afraid they aren't going to make as much money as they expect.

Kim: Forever, I have wanted to have my own business. I think my people skills would make a computer consulting business work. And I know enough about computers after all my experience.

Sharon: My friends who ran successful businesses all loved what they did. The ones who didn't were out of business in a few years.

Next Steps

This week, I want you to make two columns. In the first column, I want you to write down all of the reasons why you want to start a business. In the second column, I want you to write down all of your concerns. This comparison will help you determine whether starting a business is right for you. But finish reading the section before you make your final decision. Use the following lines to jot down your notes.

Reasons to Open a Business	Reasons not to Open a Business

52 Weeks to Well-Being:

Chapter 14

Business Structures

Many small businesses can have unanticipated pitfalls. One woman wanted to provide skin care products, but she wasn't sure how to structure the business side. She really intended to incorporate, but rapidly she became so busy that she never got around to it. Several years came and went, and then a client claimed that the product she was selling had burned his skin. He sued both the product manufacturer and her, claiming she had lied to him. Well, she hadn't, but that didn't do her any good. And worst of all, she had no corporate protection and was personally liable for all the expenses.

ONCE YOU HAVE DECIDED you want to start a business, you need to determine what business structure will be the most appropriate for you. You have several options, and there are advantages and disadvantages to each of them. Let's look at some of their major characteristics.

Sole Proprietor

Probably the easiest business structure to open is the sole proprietorship. In fact, if you take no legal steps and begin to run a business, you have chosen to be a sole proprietor by default. A sole proprietorship isn't a legal entity; instead, a sole proprietor is the owner of the business, and she is responsible for the business debt. It's possible to give the business a name other than your own, but doing so has no legal implications and offers no personal liability protections.

Sole proprietorships have some advantages. The first is that you simply decide what you want to do, obtain any certifications or licenses necessary, and begin to run your business. There is no paperwork to file with the state, and there is no business tax return. You simply report your profits and expenses on Schedule C of your personal tax return.

On the other hand, there are two major risks to a sole proprietorship. One is that you are personally responsible for any debt of the business. This means if you become over-leveraged or run into any other financial trouble, you have personal responsibility to pay back the debt.

Additionally, if your business is sued, you are also responsible for paying the lawsuit judgment amount if you lose the case. If, instead, your business was a legal entity, usually that entity would be the recipient of the suit—not you, personally. As a sole proprietor, you could lose bank accounts and even your home in the wrong situation. You will need to weigh this carefully, as anyone can be sued. Knowing this, many small businesses are still sole proprietorships. Additionally, you might begin your venture as a sole proprietorship until you determine which structure best meets your needs.

Partnerships

General partnerships are similar to sole proprietorships, except the business has two or more owners. They are easy to establish, and the business does not have a legal identity. Partnerships also have the same risks as sole proprietorships. Additionally, each partner has responsibility for the actions of the other partners. Because this is a personal risk, you should be careful before you create a partnership with someone.

A friend of mine used to tell me repeatedly to "pick my partner before I picked my project." He was always cautious when I was considering a business venture with another person. I think, over time, I have probably grown as wary as he was. Many times, I have come right up to the edge of a collaborative business project only to back away from it.

If you are considering a partnership, there are a few things to keep in mind. First, have a written agreement about the tasks and responsibilities of everyone in the partnership. This begins by discussing financial responsibilities, moves to business functions like keeping the books and paying the bills, covers any required administrative work, and then ends with how the work will be divided.

Build into your agreement what you will do if one of you fails to keep your end of the bargain. And then, finally, before you sign anything, run it by a lawyer to be sure nothing has been forgotten.

It sounds like being in business with someone else would be fun and less stressful. Sometimes it is if you pick the right partner. Otherwise, it can be a nightmare. You lose control and keep the liability. Be very careful with this arrangement.

Limited Partnerships and Limited Liability Partnerships

Limited partnerships are different from general partnerships and are quite a bit more complex and difficult to structure. In a limited partnership, there is a general partner and a limited partner (or partners). Limited partnerships are funding mechanisms. The general partners only run the business decisions and operations. The general partners also retain the liability. The limited partners only provide the financing and, in return for this, a share of the profit. Limited partners have no liability exposure; they are just investors for the general partners.

Limited liability partnerships are slightly different in that they provide limited liability for each owner. As a result, they are safer than a limited partnership for all of the members, not just the limited partners.

Limited partnerships and limited liability partnerships can be an effective way to obtain funding; however, if you are a brand-new business, you may find it difficult to find a limited partner.

You might be better served to choose a different business structure and obtain a loan from the person you were considering for the limited partnership. Then, you can pay back the loan with interest. Even then, you may discover it is difficult to find someone willing to lend the money.

Subchapter S Corporations

"S Corporations" are a popular business structure. Unlike sole proprietorships and partnerships, corporations are always legal entities. Perhaps the greatest advantage for a corporate structure is that the owner is protected from personal liability for company debts.

Additionally, the owner has greater protection in case of a lawsuit. Although individual lawsuits are always possible, a grieved party would have to "look through" the corporate structure to the individual. Such suits are unlikely to succeed.

Finally, if a business owner is attempting to raise money, shares of company stock can be sold to people willing to buy them. You might be surprised to know that these stock sales don't happen that frequently. In much the same way as new businesses are usually not limited partnerships, few people want to take the risk of purchasing your stock. Even if you find a buyer, if you are considering selling shares of your corporation, I recommend that you talk to an attorney before you make any decisions.

Remember that once you have sold a share of corporate stock, you can't get it back. You don't ever want to get into a position where you have sold so much stock that you no longer control your own business. When this happens to larger corporations, and it does from time to time, the results can be downright catastrophic. The founder of the business can find herself removed by the shareholders if she doesn't keep a majority position. Remember that owning a share of stock is the same as owning a piece of the business.

When people talk about S corporations, I don't think they really understand what they are describing. An S corporation is just a corporation. The difference is that the company makes a subchapter S tax election, which allows the profits and losses from the business to flow through to the business owner or owners rather than being retained within the corporation. Even though the S corporation has to file a tax return, there is never any income tax due because of the flow-through nature.

What does flow-through tax treatment mean, exactly? The business earns income, and it incurs expenses. These expenses may be operating, payroll, or any other costs. Once all of the bills are paid, did the business operate as a profit or a loss? This number and a few more complexities are reported on a K-1. The K-1 data is reported on the owner's tax return. If there are multiple owners, the gain/loss is divided by the share of ownership and reported on multiple K-1s.

S corporations are more complicated than sole props or partnerships to create, requiring paperwork to be filed with the state. Additionally, corporate meetings need to be held on an annual basis, and periodic state filings are required.

Limited Liability Companies (LLCs)

Limited Liability Companies are designed, as their name suggests, to help limit the liability of the business owner. LLCs have enormous flexibility and fewer business structure requirements than S corporations. They are not, however, good vehicles for trying to raise capital, as shares cannot be sold.

Additionally, taxation is an important concern when considering an LLC. First, members of an LLC are considered to be self-employed, not employees of the company, and as a result, will have to pay all of their self-employment tax liability of Medicare and Social Security rather than sharing those expenses with the entity. Additionally, LLCs can choose how they want to be taxed. They can either be taxed as a sole proprietor (if it's one person) or a partnership (if it's owned by multiple people). If they prefer, the LLC can also be taxed as an S corporation, filing a separate return but retaining flow-through tax treatment.

So as you are trying to decide which business entity to select, you should start with two questions. The first question is "Do I need protection from lawsuits?" If so, you don't want to select a sole proprietorship or a partnership, as both of these entities cause you to retain all that risk. Then, the next question is, "How am I going to raise the funds to get my business off the ground?" If you are planning to sell shares, then you probably want to select a corporation with a subchapter S election. To facilitate fund raising, you could also consider a limited partnership, but an LLC is likely a bad choice.

Once you have established your business structure, it's usually possible to make changes, but you really don't want to have to do that. Take a little time now, talk to your attorney, CPA, and financial planner to learn the details, and look at the advantages and disadvantages of each business structure. Then, choose the one that seems most likely to help you meet your goals.

Megan: I would like to start a business, but I think it makes more sense for me to get an associate's degree first. I don't think I'm financially secure enough to take the risk of a business failing, and no one would lend me money.

Jessica: I remember studying different kinds of business structures in college. What I remember the most is how complicated it is and how much research someone should complete before they choose.

Kim: Even if I take all the right steps, someone might sue me if they thought I compromised their personal data through a computer repair. I think I need a business structure with some kind of protection.

Sharon: I wish people weren't so quick to sue. Personal liability always scares me.

Next Steps

Take some time to review potential business structures, and discuss your tax and legal situations with your CPA, attorney, and financial planner. Don't delay the decision on your business entity. As you grow in your business, you will have less and less time for analysis. Use the following chart as a template, then use the following lines to jot down your notes.

Business Structure	Advantages	Disadvantages
Sole Proprietor		
Partnership		
Limited (Liability) Partnership		
S Corporation		
Limited Liability Company (LLC)		

Chapter 15

Steps in Writing a Business Plan

Every time the business owners of the new consulting firm thought they had accounted for all the bills, something else seemed to emerge. They understood both the expenses and income of their venture, but clients were harder to acquire, and the bills kept mounting. They came to me for advice, and I suggested they begin by changing their focus from acquiring clients to creating a business plan. It didn't have to be fancy or difficult, but they needed something to guide their decisions.

MANY PEOPLE ARE afraid to create a business plan. The task isn't really difficult, but the process can be brutal. A business plan shows the strengths and weaknesses of a new venture, and people sometimes prefer to fly blind than to address downfalls they may experience. However, even if you are apprehensive, create the plan. If you discover many weaknesses, you don't have to give up on your idea. Just knowing the potential pitfalls can help you create solutions that will lead to long-term success.

Although business plans can take many forms, they tend to have some similar components. As you address each section, take some time to think about your responses. The more detailed your business plan, the more it is likely to provide you with useful information.

Executive Summary

In the executive summary, you create an overview description of your business. It will include a brief overview of important components, but it won't go into great detail on how they are executed. Think of it as a view from 50,000 feet.

Company Description

The company description will include your business structure. It will also talk about the ways your business can earn money, and it might include any business or industry constraints you may need to address. The company description is more revenue and regulatory focused than the executive summary. It's also a great place for you to describe your passion for your new venture.

Organization and Management

Here you'll describe how your business is organized, and why you chose your business structure. You also identify your business officers and why they were chosen. You will also want to explain any other levels of management. Where the company description just listed your business structure, here you talk about it in greater detail.

Services or Products

Explain the details of what you are selling or the service you're providing and why it is different than your competition. You must be able to answer why the existing market needs you to enter the space.

Market Analysis

Many people in marketing say that knowing your ideal customer is critical to business success. You must describe who wants your products or services and what actions you can take to be more appealing. Remember that if you aren't sure of the details, provide what you know or suspect and modify it over time.

Marketing and Sales Plan

Your marketing and sales plan is closely related to answering the question of why the market needs you to enter it. You will need to work from your strengths and convince your customers (or sources of financing) that any weaknesses should not be troubling. In today's competitive world, you will likely need a physical presence and an online presence that includes a website and social media. Look at your target audience and focus your marketing plan around where you think they shop.

Funding Request

If you are writing your plan as an effort to obtain funding, then you should be clear about what you need. Do adequate analysis before you ask for funds. You may have trouble obtaining a "yes," and you want to be sure you have enough money for your business to both survive and thrive.

Financial Projections

Of course, it will be much easier to obtain funding if you have reasonable data that shows your financial projections for your firm. These numbers should not be wishful thinking but instead solidly researched expectations that you really believe you can meet.

Appendix

The appendix includes any other data and documents you need to support your plan, like resumes, licenses, permits, etc.

So that's the overview of your business plan. Don't let the formality of it overwhelm you. Once you know what you need in your plan, the next step is determining how you will address the questions described above. It can be daunting, so break it into small pieces and focus your work around researching and networking.

To create a business plan, you must become an expert on your enterprise. Fortunately, today, much of the data that you need is available online. However, there is a lot of wrong information on the internet as well! It's human nature to be drawn to articles that confirm what we want to be true, so you need to be objective and check your sources.

Nevertheless, it's probably easiest to begin by doing an internet search on the company you are wanting to franchise into or into the field you are entering. Read everything. Once you have exhausted online material, look for journals or even possibly books that provide details and specifics. Also, remember to look at articles that are critical of your idea! You need to try to decide whether or not the criticisms are warranted.

Next, spend considerable time talking to people who are already in your field. People are usually very generous in giving advice. The idea that business life is a "dog eat dog" world can be true to some extent, but you will find many gracious people who don't see you as competition. Instead, they see you as another small business owner trying to make good decisions, and they are happy to help you succeed.

Online communities exist, but unless you are running only an online business, you also need to get to know the leaders in your own community.

When I opened my firm, I was surprised that there was a different "business world" in the town where I had lived for years. Begin to enter this world by joining your Chamber of Commerce. Then, once you are a member, go to the events and get to know people.

I know it can be difficult to describe yourself as a business owner the first few times. That's okay. Keep doing it, and it will get easier over time. Once you begin this process, it puts you into the position to meet other business owners, people who are in your profession who may be able to assist you as you formalize your business plan. These folks will know the hidden costs you aren't seeing and may offer tips on how to improve your business processes.

Once you have researched your vocation, you might think you are done, but you're not! You still have to take the time to learn how to run a business. I absolutely believe that most small businesses don't fail because the people aren't good at what they do. The businesses go under because working "in" a business is very different than working "on" a business. I know that keeping books, running payroll, and preparing taxes is not what you want to be doing. However, accurate financials are an important component of your business plan, so you need to learn how to create them, even if you make the decision later to outsource the tasks.

Additionally, you won't want to outsource much at first because money will be tight. This is such a disappointment to the new business owner. Unfortunately, your potential customers were probably functioning successfully before you arrived. It's up to you to change their mind and make your business indispensable to their lives. But it takes time. The kiss of death for your baby business is to overly extend your cash flow. Anything you do yourself, you don't have to pay someone else to do.

Finally, as you prepare to share your business plan, structure it to be appealing to your readers. If you are seeking financing, then you will want to take the time to show the economic viability of your project. If you are trying to attract customers, then you want to focus on your product and why it is special. Most of all, however, your business plan is written for you. You are the most important audience. Look at everything objectively—the financial costs, the marketing issues, the supplies you will need, and finally the potential for a market. Only then can you decide whether or not this new venture can work for you right now.

Megan: A business plan seems to be a lot of the secret to business success.

Jessica: I wish I were an entrepreneur, but I just hate risk too much.

Kim: I've dreaded a business plan because I thought I didn't know enough to write one. These steps don't seem so bad, and I think I can find the information.

Sharon: The most important part of creating a business plan is deciding what you want to do. I've seen people who wanted to own consulting firms, but I could never figure out what they were consulting about!

Next Steps

START YOUR BUSINESS PLAN. Feel free to begin with easier parts, like your passion for your business, or why you think you have a great idea. Then, research your new venture in as much detail as possible. Finally, join local community groups so you can begin to interact with other business owners. Jot some notes on the following lines.

_____

_____

_____

_____

_____

Chapter 16

Financial Statements

I see it happen all the time. A hopeful entrepreneur opens a new business—maybe a restaurant or a retail shop. Business isn't great, but it's good. From the outside, I'm optimistic because the owners seem knowledgeable. However, within a couple of years, the doors are closed. Financially, the business just couldn't survive, and the owner who was great at the business didn't know how to run it.

KEEPING business financials is critically important even though they are not exciting, and the process can be difficult at first. However, your financials are the fastest way to see the progress you are making. If that doesn't make you enthusiastic, then know that your financial records will also provide you with information on how to lower your taxes. Let's look at some of them in more detail.

Cash Flow Statement

Your cash flow is probably the most important document for you to maintain and review regularly. It is exactly what it sounds like. Assuming you are operating from a "cash basis" on your taxes (not an accrual basis), to calculate your cash flow, you list all of your income and all of your expenses for a determined period of time. Then, you classify the income and expenses, likely using some form of accounting software. Even if you work with an accountant who keeps your books and records for you, I recommend you help her with the classification of your expenses. You should have a good understanding of the money you are earning and where that money is going.

Once you have the income listed (usually at the top of the report) and the expenses listed below it, you subtract the expenses from the income. You want the results to be positive!

Other than the obvious importance of knowing whether or not you are operating in the red, your cash flow statement offers other interesting insights. First, you can track the progression of your income. You want to see steady growth until it reaches the level you want to sustain.

Additionally, when you look at all your monthly expenses on one page, you can review them and see if they are necessary. It is easy to acquire subscriptions and expenses over time and never realize you don't use the services. Periodically, look at what you spend very critically. Do you really need to buy all that stuff? Are you using it? Is there a cheaper, or even better, free alternative?

Finally, your cash flow statement is a good way to estimate your tax liability, although tax consequences may also be adjusted by a few balance sheet items discussed below, like depreciation. Your taxable income is basically what is left after you have paid your bills. To have an accurate cash flow, remember to keep all your receipts along with proof of your income—cash records, maybe copies of checks, and credit card payment summaries.

Depreciation

Depreciation is a schedule where you take expenses over a period of time rather than all at once. This allows you to smooth your expenses and lower your income in future years when your earnings may be higher. However, remember that it is possible to deduct even very costly items, like computers and furniture, all at once. This would lower your tax liability for that year, although it could result in higher taxes in subsequent years.

Profit/Loss Statement

In the unlikely event that you aren't keeping your books on a cash basis and, instead, you keep your books on an accrual basis, you will also want to keep a profit/loss statement. Accrual accounting is more complicated than cash accounting. Briefly, in accrual accounting, expenses aren't recognized in the month they occur, and income isn't recognized totally in the month it is earned. As a result, with accrual accounting the profit/loss statement serves the same purpose as the cash flow statement.

Balance Sheet

Where a cash flow or profit/loss statement is created for a period of time, like a month or year, a balance sheet is calculated for a specific moment in time. Your balance sheet lists all your assets and all your liabilities on a page. The difference between assets and liabilities is called "owner's equity," and you want it to be a positive number.

Your assets are categorized as current or fixed. Current assets are cash or items that could be converted to cash within a year. Fixed assets are items that you don't plan to sell, like furniture, equipment, and items necessary to run your business. Fixed assets can also include land and buildings.

Liabilities also have two categories: short-term liabilities and long-term debt. Short-term liabilities are items like accounts payable or taxes you owe. Long-term debt is bank loans or money owed to shareholders. If you don't have shareholders, then your long-term debt is money you borrowed that you don't anticipate having paid in full within twelve months.

Even though balance sheets show a moment in time, you probably don't need to calculate one frequently unless it is required for regulatory reasons. Instead, you want to track your changes in owner's equity over time. As your owner's equity number increases, you will see your business moving to a more stable financial place. Some tax returns require a balance sheet, so you will want to create at least one balance sheet a year unless something requires that you create one more regularly.

In summary, your cash flow statement shows money in/money out. Your balance sheet shows the value of your assets and liabilities. For example, your cash flow statement will show items like the money you made from a recent sale and your rent payment. Your balance sheet includes the value of your computer and the loan you took out to get your business started. All the data is valuable, but it is very different.

Bank Reconciliation

I know that reconciling your bank statement may be something you've avoided for years even before you had a business. However, knowing how much money is in your bank account and how your money moves in and out of your account is important for your business' financial security. Primarily, it will keep you from bouncing checks. One bounced check is not the end of the world, but when you bounce checks on a regular basis, you pay money in fees, lower your credit score, and ding your reputation.

Some professions require bank reconciliations. For instance, financial advisers are required to keep them because it provides the easiest way for regulators to check for money laundering or embezzlement. Your use of a bank reconciliation is probably simpler than that, but it is still important.

You may need to keep additional financial statements other than the ones discussed here, and you may be thinking that you will use your first positive cash flow to pay someone else to create these documents. Still, I want you to take the time to review them. If you understand your business' financial circumstances, you can make adjustments before you go too far off track. A good knowledge of whether or not you are making money gives you tools you can use to keep your business profitable or make corrections.

Megan: I would hate to have to keep all these records.

Jessica: I need to reconcile my bank statements even outside of owning a business. I track my spending mentally, but this would stop me from making a mistake.

Kim: I'm much more worried about my cash flow than I am about my net worth for my consulting firm. I need to earn enough to replace my salary if I try to do this full time.

Sharon: As my husband and I became more successful, we tracked our progress by calculating our net worth about four times a year.

Next Steps

Enough stalling. Take some time and organize your financial records. If you hate it, schedule some time in your planner, like a meeting. Take one hour a week and create or review your financial documents. Just one hour a week won't disrupt your schedule, even if you are busy. Within three months, you will be proud of how organized you are! Jot your ideas on the following lines.

Chapter 17

Payroll and Payroll Taxes

I always wonder about the people on the ads who suddenly owe the IRS tens of thousands of dollars with, apparently, no warning. The tax reduction services they hawk concern me almost as much as wondering how they miscalculated their taxes so extensively. Were they small business owners who earned more than they expected?

WE ALL LOVE to get paychecks! However, when you are the one who has to calculate payroll, you may find you dread getting paid every month. Remember that when you calculate payroll, you have to keep several taxes in mind.

Withholding income tax on the state and federal level is one part of calculating payroll. Fortunately, the percentage to be withheld is actually chosen by the employee. Of course, you may be an employee of your company, too, depending on the business structure you have chosen, and as such, you will withhold your own taxes.

Income tax isn't your only tax liability, however. I know many business consultants encourage owners to dodge the position of "employee" as much as possible. Instead, they want you to take a "draw" or "distribution" and avoid payroll taxes. Payroll taxes are comprised of payments to fund Unemployment and Social Security. However, I think being an employee is a good status. When you are an employee and take a traditional paycheck, you are automatically funding a Social Security pension for yourself every month.

Additionally, the IRS expects you to take a salary in addition to the draw. If the business takes the structure of an LLC, then the owner is not an employee and doesn't have as much obligation to take a salary. Even so, she still has to pay Social Security and Unemployment through self-employment taxes.

I take a pretty optimistic view of Social Security, believing that no individual session of Congress will be willing to eliminate the benefit. Because of this, I'm a fan of your funding a Social Security benefit for yourself. Additionally, if you have paid into Unemployment, you can actually claim on it if your business fails. To earn the benefit, you need to pay yourself a salary, so those safeguards are available to you, just like every other employee in your firm. It seems obvious, but I see people make the mistake often—they don't want to pay into Social Security, and then they're upset when they aren't earning a benefit!

There's another use for Unemployment, as well. Sometimes, you and your spouse may own a business together. I have seen situations where the couple divorces, and one spouse keeps the business. This can cause the other spouse no longer to have a job in the company. If both of you have paid your payroll taxes, the unemployed spouse can make a claim. If you haven't paid into Unemployment, you can't take the benefit.

Employment taxes are paid by both the employer and the employee, half and half. So for yourself, you will need to pay the half for the employee and the half for the employer.

When you are self-employed and taking payroll, you should anticipate losing quite a bit of your gross pay to taxes between payroll, federal, and state liabilities.

Theoretically, it's not that difficult to calculate income tax, Social Security, and Unemployment tax liabilities. However, determining the amount is the easy part. Then you must enter the correct amounts on the appropriate forms and send them in to the appropriate agencies. Finally, periodic reports also need to be filed.

If your business focuses on accounting, you may think that all of this sounds like fun. For the rest of us, even intrepid financial planners, we look at all the requirements, and we begin to run backwards.

As a result, even if you are the only employee in your company, I strongly recommend that you use a payroll service. A payroll service takes care of all of these responsibilities for you. They come at different price levels, but general payroll processing is quite affordable. With the IRS scrutiny and penalties that come with payroll errors, strongly consider outsourcing this part of your business. I'm a fan of doing much of your work yourself, but payroll might be best left to another expert.

~

Megan: I have friends who work independently at contract-style jobs. I don't think they are paying self-employment taxes. They need to read this.

Jessica: I had to make an adjustment to my tax withholding when I still owed money at the end of the year!

Kim: I had a friend tell me that I would lose 50% of my income if I were self-employed. I'm not sure it will be quite that high, but it will be close.

Sharon: I've seen so many people need unemployment benefits who never thought it could happen to them. I think it's risky to avoid paying into those social insurance systems.

Next Steps

As you try to decide how to handle your payroll and tax withholding, I strongly recommend you talk to a CPA and hire a payroll service. I know you want to save money, but payroll is complicated, and the IRS penalties for errors can be expensive. Jot your ideas on the following lines.

Chapter 18

Small Business Retirement Plans

When the gift shop first opened, there was almost no cash flow. The owner was always relieved when she could pay her rent. But business improved, and soon, Berta's Birthday Baskets became the talk of the town. She had several employees and really wanted both to save for her own retirement and be kind to her staff. She thought that creating a retirement plan would be a useful benefit for all of them.

WHEN YOU WORK FOR YOURSELF, you don't have the luxury of just enrolling in your employer's plan. Instead, it's up to you to choose the type of retirement plan that will be most appropriate for your business. This chapter looks at the characteristics of SEP IRAs, SIMPLE IRAs, and 401(k)s from the perspective of the business owner.

Small business retirement plans have different strengths and weaknesses, and it is important for you, the business owner, to understand the ease of implementation, cost, and required employer contributions before you make a selection. Additionally, the amount of money that can be deferred is different, so you need to select the plan that allows you to adequately fund your own retirement need.

Remember that traditional IRAs and Roth IRAs are not included in this chapter, as they are not small business retirement plans and have been previously covered in the first section of the book.

Simplified Employee Pension (SEP) IRAs are easy and inexpensive to establish. However, SEP IRAs are funded only through employer contributions. This means that employees cannot defer money into a SEP on their own behalf. As a result, you need to consider whether or not you want to provide all of the funds for the retirement benefit or whether you want to encourage employee participation.

The biggest advantage of the SEP is the amount that can be contributed. In 2023, an employer can contribute 25% of compensation, up to $66,000. As a result, if you own a business and you are the only employee, the SEP provides an excellent, inexpensive tool to defer large amounts of money into your own retirement account.

If you have employees, however, remember that you will have to fund their accounts at the same level as your own. I had an employer once who wanted to fund his SEP at one percentage and his employees' accounts at a lower level. You can't do that.

Additionally, most of your employees will qualify for the plan. The minimum participation level for a SEP is an employee who is at least twenty-one years old, who worked for you three out of the last five years, and who has earned at least $600 per year. The income level will exclude practically no one; the only limiting factor is the years of service. By the way, it doesn't matter whether you categorize your employees as full time or part time; the amount of money is the only consideration.

Because the SEP is an IRA-based account, it has a few additional wrinkles. First, employees are instantly vested in any contributions. So if you fund an account and the employee quits the next day, the money is theirs to take. Additionally, you cannot take a loan from a SEP, as IRAs don't allow loans. And finally, there are required minimum distributions (RMDs) that begin at age seventy-two or later (depending on your current age), even if you are still employed. (Remember that the SECURE and SECURE 2.0 Acts passed at the end of 2019 and 2022 changed the age that RMDs begin.) Sometimes, this results in contributions into a plan the same year as distributions. This isn't as confusing in practice as it sounds here, but the penalty can be painful if the RMDs aren't taken.

A second retirement plan option is the SIMPLE IRA. SIMPLEs are also easy and inexpensive to establish and can be a good choice for small business owners with employees.

SIMPLE IRAs can be funded by the employees up to $15,500 in 2023 with a $3,500 catch up if the employee is fifty or older. On top of that, the employer either offers a nonelective contribution or a match. A nonelective contribution does not require any employee participation, and it must be 2% of compensation. The match is 3% of compensation, but it can be reduced to 1% of compensation two out of five years. That way, if the business has some financial difficulties, the employer responsibility can be quite low for a significant length of time.

It's slightly harder to qualify for a SIMPLE than a SEP, but most employees will still be eligible. Rather than $600 of annual income, SIMPLEs require $5,000 worth of annual income in any prior two years with an expectation of $5,000 in the current year. Again, it doesn't matter whether the employer categorizes the employee as full or part time. It's based on the amount of money earned.

In addition to instant vesting, SIMPLEs have a few other peculiar characteristics you should know. First, they are only available for companies that have a hundred or fewer employees. Additionally, if you offer a SIMPLE plan, you cannot also offer another kind of retirement plan. This sounds like a burden, but I'm betting you really aren't wanting to set up two different retirement plans!

SIMPLE plans not only prohibit loans, but they also prohibit employees from taking distributions during the first two years of plan participation. This causes the biggest issues if you open a SIMPLE for your business and you have older employees. Like other IRAs, SIMPLEs have RMD requirements for all employees. As a result, don't open a plan if an employee will be required to take an RMD and yet can't take a distribution from the plan because it is within the first two-year restriction. I saw this error once. I inherited the problem that was caused by the previous adviser, and it was a nightmare to sort out with the IRS.

Finally, I want to talk a little about a 401(k) plan, because these are the plans that everyone assumes will be opened. However, on closer examination, two issues become obvious fairly quickly. First, even reasonably priced 401(k) plans are quite expensive. Next, the paperwork requirements can be overwhelming. I'm not suggesting that you shouldn't have a 401(k) plan, but you should know what's involved.

Although many employees are eligible for 401(k) participation, the requirements are stricter. Employees must be at least twenty-one years old and have worked 1,000 hours the previous year. Just a note here—it's always possible for an employer to waive these requirements and allow 401(k) participation as soon as an employee is hired. She just can't require the employees to meet a stricter set of standards, and of course, the requirements have to be the same for all employees.

It's also possible to allow loans within 401(k) plans, along with distributions for hardship or other qualifying events. For employees who want to take advantage of these options, they must make a request to the plan administrator.

The biggest advantages the 401(k) provides to the business owner are the ability to defer considerable resources out of her salary and the ability to put a vesting schedule onto the company contributions. Let's look at the funding first.

In 2023, any employee can defer $22,500, and if she is over fifty, she can defer an additional $7,500. If the employer wants to defer the maximum amounts into her own account, she must offer either a match or a nonelective contribution to her employees. Without these actions, the employer will be limited in her funding amounts. The details are complicated, so talk to your financial planner for implementation strategies.

Employees are always vested in the money they defer into the 401(k) plan from their own pay, but there can be a vesting schedule for employer contributions. This vesting can occur all at once after an allowed period of time (called cliff vesting) or as percentages over time (called graded vesting).

I would strongly encourage you to consult with your company's CPA, financial planner, and possibly attorney to be sure that your 401(k) plan is drafted correctly, and you are following all of the rules accurately. Small business owners make huge mistakes in 401(k) plans every year, and you don't want to have to deal with the Department of Labor or the IRS.

Retirement plans are great for company morale and make your company an attractive and competitive choice for top talent. Just be sure you make a decision that works within your company's current financial situation.

> Megan: I want a better job with a retirement plan.

> Jessica: I am really glad my company offers a 401(k) plan with a match. I think a small business would need to be financially secure before they tried something like that.

> Kim: Even though I never intend to hire an employee, I would rather have a SIMPLE than a SEP just in case my plans change in the future.

> Sharon: The discussion about these plans is interesting, but I believe the most important piece is to save money for retirement. Do it any way you want but start saving because it's here before you know it.

Next Steps

The IRS is a great source of information for small business owners. Begin by going to IRS.gov and reviewing Publication 3998 for a discussion of different kinds of plans and their requirements and tax consequences. The document is easy to read, and it should be available as a PDF for you to download or read online. Then, consult your accountant and financial planner for the details about the plan that would best help you meet your needs. Jot some notes on the following lines.

. . .

Chapter 19

Creating Your Brand

When I was twelve or thirteen and attending the theater, I read the programs cover to cover. I was amazed that if you owned a business, you could have your name in the program as someone who supported the event. I thought those people and their firms must be remarkable. Years later, the first advertisement I purchased was in support of a local university's theater season. I wanted my business to be seen as assisting their effort. Over time, I have broadened my backing to other organizations, and I love supporting our local art events.

As YOU WERE COMPLETING your business plan in the earlier chapter, part of it asked you to anticipate your marketing efforts. However, before you can market or advertise, you need to decide how you want your firm or service to be viewed. With words and images, you must condense what you do and what unique qualities you bring to your business that set you apart from your competitors. In other words, create a brand.

If you have purchased a franchise or are serving as a representative for another company (like a makeup manufacturer or a chain restaurant), then the company's main positions have already been established for you. You might want to take time to look into the company's practices to be sure they are a good fit. Once you've done your research, you will still have some branding opportunities—you can put your own "face" on your product. The easiest way to do this is to tell the story of what brought you to the business. If you don't have a personal story about what you do, then do some research into the firm, so you can talk compellingly about it. If you don't care about your business, you will have a difficult time being successful.

There's nothing wrong with choosing a career because it is lucrative or easy to fit into your schedule. However, convenience won't be compelling to your clients or customers, so you need to create a better story. Your story should be true, and it should feel authentic. I've seen people in all lines of work. Assuming the product is of reasonable quality, the person who sells it seems to make more of a difference than the item itself. If you only see your venture as a way to make money, you won't be successful, so find a passion. Not only will it help your sales, but it will also increase your personal satisfaction.

If you are creating an independent business, you probably have the passion, so that problem is solved. However, your branding decisions are more critical. No one has ever heard of your business, so why should they use you? Shop there? Avail themselves of your service? The answers to these questions will help you define your brand.

What is your product or service, and what do you want people to think of and feel when they consider what you offer? That's the essence of your brand. It's more than what you provide. The service itself impacts how you want people to view it. If it's a gift shop, you might want people to think that it is the place to go to find that special gift or the place to go where someone is always ready with suggestions to meet your shopping needs. If you have an insurance agency, you may want to be seen as solid and ready to help when things go wrong.

If your business brand is exactly what people expect to see, you may be reassuring, but you may not be very memorable. On the other hand, if you jar them more than they expect, you might turn them off. Although I want the meeting with my insurance agent to be pleasant, I'm more interested in outcome than experience. I want the product to meet my need, and I want to believe that my agent is providing me with good, dependable service.

The most important part of your brand is you! "What do people think about when they think about you?" In a small business, this step is vital, as you will become somewhat interchangeable with your business. As a result, it's a good practice that if you sell a product, you should use it yourself.

Sometimes your brand can be challenging. For example, when I tell people I am in financial services, people begin to move away. Then I tell them the story of how I entered the business because of my mother's horrible experiences with a stockbroker. After that, I frame myself as someone who helps people gain control of their money. People like that. Finally, I go into my characteristics that distinguish me from my competitors and show I'm competent. By explaining my motivation, describing my services as something most people need, and defining myself as the best person to provide it because I act as a fiduciary, I've created a brand.

Your brand is also the experience of doing business with you. This has multiple components. Initially, it is the physical environment of your store or office. What is the first impression someone would have as they entered the space? This is where your branding decisions become important. What's in the window? Does your gift shop smell like cinnamon potpourri? Have you designed the space to be impressive or comfortable? Is the coffee fresh and the bathroom clean? Does someone greet customers and offer to help them when they walk into the office or store? All of this is your brand!

Perhaps your office doesn't hold a physical space but exists online. Now you don't have a store—instead, you have a website. That's fine, and it's becoming more and more common. But it puts a lot of pressure on the site. For some people, your website will be the most important aspect of your brand. In the next chapter, we're going to expand the discussion of brand to include social media and online marketing.

The final part of creating your brand is a general sense of how people think about the entire package you are offering. I know you don't have any money—heck, at this point you probably don't even have the business yet. However, the more you can plug into your community, the easier it will be for you to get customers and clients.

Years ago, I made the decision to be a business that supported community activities. In fact, I sponsor events much more than I advertise—my thirteen-year-old self would approve. The nice thing about being a small sponsor of your town's music festival is that people see your name or the name of your business throughout the event. It's advertising, but you're actually doing something for someone else rather than just asking for something. Advertising is fine, but look for opportunities to promote your brand and business in more creative ways as well.

If you're not a public relations or marketing major, creating a brand can feel phony and artificial. You may want to call in an expert. Be careful, though, if you hire someone to help you promote your business. They should be well versed and professional. Some firms may hold themselves out as experts but only have some general skills or strategies in one area. Remember to ask for references and check out their qualifications.

If you opt to run your own promotional campaigns, put yourself in the shoes of your client or customer. Where do you want to shop or meet? Who do you want to talk to? What kind of experience would leave you happy? What needs do you have? Answering these questions will help you define a brand that you can sustain over time.

Megan: It's amazing how brand reputation makes a difference. Sometimes, the products are the same, but people may favor one store over another.

Jessica: I love the position my company takes on issues like recycling and micro loans for women in other countries. I'm proud to be part of their brand.

Kim: I'm not sure people expect their IT expert to be a woman. I'll bet I could create a good brand around that.

Sharon: I think creating a brand is tricky. I've seen companies market themselves as ethical and honest, and then they don't act that way. The consumers notice.

Next Steps

What makes your company unique? Special? What do you

bring to your career that sets you apart? What do you want people to think about when they think of you? Now brainstorm strategies or activities that would help you create this brand within your business. Jot your ideas on the following lines.

Chapter 20

Social Media and Advertising

The other day I was looking for a feed store to purchase hay for my horse. I had heard of a company in Oklahoma City, but there was some confusion over its name. The store didn't have a website or well-designed social media pages. I also discovered that the online address service I use has begun to charge a fee. Eventually I found the store and bought the hay. However, my frustration level was high.

Marketing today is nothing like your grandparents' marketing. Not very long ago, having an ad in the Yellow Pages was one of the first expenses a new business needed to cover. Today most people don't even bother to pick up paper phone books when they are available. The giant volume has been replaced with an app on your phone. Many newspapers are having trouble maintaining readership, and print magazines are getting rare.

As a result, most of the older books published on marketing and advertising are ineffective in today's world. Too, the sheer volume of messages that bombard people daily makes it difficult to snag their attention so that they will consider doing business with you. As a result, some of the most challenging decisions you will need to make early in your business venture will focus on how to promote, publicize, advertise, and market your service or product. Take the time to think through your options rather than throwing significant money randomly at this or that campaign. You need to decide what forums will get your message to people who might be interested in your product and service and then put together a coordinated plan.

Of course, "significant money" is however you define it. When you are getting started, small sums can be daunting, but as your business grows, you will find that your promotion budget will increase. It can be frustrating to realize you will have the most money to acquire customers and clients after your business is running well.

Receptive audiences are either audiences that are genuinely interested in what you are offering, or they are so bored that they will read literally anything. This is why, for example, advertising in playbills (like I described in the last chapter) can be effective. However, I learned this from the school of hard knocks.

I had been in business a short time when the phone rang. Someone on the other end of the call had heard of my business, and they thought they had found a great opportunity to help me find clients. I didn't know this meant my name was on a list. As the salesperson asked a couple of leading questions, I provided more information than I realized at the time. Suddenly this rep had the perfect product for me.

So what was the once in a lifetime offer the sales rep had for me, the new financial planner? It was an advertising opportunity at a popular work-out facility. For $2,000 I would be featured on a bulletin board. I could leave flyers and cards. Did I know that in my hometown, many doctors, attorneys, and other professionals who would need a financial planner went to that gym? Many times a week?

I would love to tell you that I laughed at the guy and hung up the phone, but I really thought he chose me. Yes, I know. Sucker.... So I spent $2,000 and had my new ad at the trendy gym. Do you know how many clients I got from that disaster? None. Zero. All I did was spend my money. It's true--many of my town's doctors are members of this gym. The problem for me is that NONE of them went to the gym looking for a financial planner! They were focused on getting to the track, on the machines, or in the pool. They didn't even see my bulletin board poster. They just walked by it on their way to their interest.

It was a great lesson. I have found that it's much better to focus your advertising in places where people are reading closely.

Better than buying an ad in a local newspaper or magazine is to have someone feature you in an article, or even provide the content yourself. This is another place where your local Chamber of Commerce can help. Generally, they will have events focused around the time of your business opening. Not only does this get people into your office, but the Chamber will also feature your ribbon cutting on their website. And suddenly a few people have heard of you!

I talked in the last chapter about my decision to sponsor events rather than purchase much advertising. However, I still do purchase the occasional ad. There is a place for paper advertisements in today's world because not everyone who might be interested in your service or product is active online.

However, an online presence is an important, affordable way for people to learn who you are.

In the past, a website was enough. Unfortunately, today your website is just the beginning. A successful online presence involves at least your website, social media accounts, and content that you either create or acquire that is compelling to readers.

So how do you keep from becoming overwhelmed? First, unlike the recent Academy Award-winning movie, you can't be *Everything, Everywhere, All at Once*. Take some time to study the different social media sites, and try to decide where your audience has plugged in or what forums give you the best way to showcase your products or services. For instance, right now there is a site where people focus on crafts and projects. I don't have a social media presence on this page. Yes, people who like crafts probably need financial planning, but I would only try to place something on this site if it drew a connection between crafting and financial planning.

Don't just trust your own opinion of a site. Study the demographics of the users. You may need to branch out of your comfort zone, but that's okay. It increases the size of your digital footprint.

This leads to the next question—should you have separate social media accounts for your personal posts and your business posts? I suggest that if you are trying to look professional, you may not want to mix business posts with pictures of you in casual attire while you're on vacation at the beach.

I have multiple pages. In fact, I separate personal social media, media for my planning firm, and media for my writing and speaking events. Part of this is regulatory, and part is my desire to keep the businesses separate. It's a little more work, but I think it's worth it.

Once you have chosen your platforms, take time to create good social media posts. It's fine to repost articles, but you should also create your own posts and include original comments and content. Be careful with the privacy of anyone in your pictures, especially children.

Try to offer posts that don't just ask people to do business with you. I've heard that you should create a ratio of about one to seven. For each post where you ask someone for their business, you want to post something they find genuinely interesting seven times. Now, I think if you sell products, some of these seven posts can certainly feature those products. But even then, try to branch out and create posts that relate to your business but aren't specifically requests for customers.

Additionally, don't create one post and copy it directly onto all of your social media accounts every single time. People follow you on different platforms because they are trying to see different sides of what you offer or to learn about you in different ways. Yes, cross posting is fine to an extent, but try to offer at least some unique content on each forum.

In addition to social media sites, should you keep a blog? It depends on what you do and how much you like to write. Of course, blogs can have pictures, graphics, and other multi-media. The biggest advantage to the blog is it almost guarantees that you are creating original content.

Another way of creating content is through a podcast. Podcasts have become popular as people can listen to episodes while they are driving, exercising, or completing other tasks. If you don't currently listen to podcasts, subscribe to several. Some should be in your field, and some should offer podcasting tips. Additionally, invest in a good microphone, and tape in a place that has good acoustics. Don't be intimidated by the sound of your own voice!

All the marketing seminars I have attended over the last couple of years have focused on creating content. But I would like to offer a few disclaimers, so your efforts have the desired effect.

First, it's great to decide that you are an expert in a field, but your reader may want a little more than just your word for it. Why are you an expert? What do you know about this topic that gives you a unique perspective and ability to share your opinions with the world? One of the drawbacks of blogging and social media is that it inflates our sense of self-importance. And yet the best part of social media is the ability to hear the thoughts of smart people in almost real time. You want to provide that kind of content. Whatever you do, try to gain the knowledge to be the expert on it. Additionally, you need to be entertaining. Make people look forward to your content. If you are both knowledgeable and engaging, your social media will be a hit!

Finally, boosting posts is a good way to be sure your ideas are being seen. One advantage of social media marketing is the relatively low cost of boosting posts and running advertisements. One ad in the newspaper can cost a few hundred dollars—one ad! That kind of budget could allow you to boost social media posts for several months. Don't magnify every post. Only boost those things that you want people to see many times. I know that at first, it's difficult to make those distinctions, so pay attention to your own social media consumption.

Successfully promoting your business can be difficult. You may want to work with a public relations specialist, one who is skilled in all the tools available to establish your business in the hearts and minds of the public. Alternately, seek out individuals who have a track record for producing results in your industry. But first take some time to try to create your own strategies. Remember that cash flow is critical for small businesses. Spending too much at first can be disastrous.

Megan: I've seen so many friends get in trouble at work over what they posted on their social media. I try to tell them never to complain about their job. Your supervisor can read your posts.

Jessica: Sometimes, social media advertisements annoy me, but I have to admit that I've purchased several products because the ads were on my feed.

Kim: I need a great website if I'm going to promote myself as an IT expert. I don't understand people who have sites with broken links.

Sharon: Some companies believe that older adults aren't active online. I have a few friends who avoid it, but many of us check sites daily. We're an important and growing group, and sometimes people ignore us.

Next Steps

If you don't have a website for your business, create one. Do it yourself, or look for website companies that have designed sites you find pleasing. Such companies may or may not be in your own community, but today, it's easy to do business across state lines. You should also research different social media platforms to decide which ones reach your potential clients. You will want a social media presence, but don't spread your-self so thin you don't have time to post regularly. Keep your notes on the following lines.

Chapter 21

Hiring Employees

A young veterinarian had a successful practice. As she grew in size, she hired a great assistant. Then she didn't want as many mundane responsibilities, so she paid other people to feed and walk the dogs. Her first hire was amazing, but the other employees worked more slowly and demanded more money. Soon, much of her income was spent on payroll. Ultimately, her payroll and overhead were so out of hand that she was forced to close.

MANY PEOPLE who own a business have no intention of hiring employees. However, over time business needs may change and grow. Some businesses may need employees immediately. Good employees are tremendously valuable, but poor hiring choices can bring a business down. Being careful in your hiring process can lead to more success.

First, why are you hiring employees? Do you have more work than you can accomplish by yourself? Would hiring an employee free you up to earn more money because you no longer need to accomplish administrative tasks? These are great reasons to hire someone.

Remember, though, that once you hire an employee, you will need to find the money to pay him or her each month. If there are limited funds, the employee will get paid before you do. Are you okay with that?

Additionally, if an employee really isn't working out, do you feel comfortable with the idea of firing him or her? Really think about the answer to this question. It can be difficult, and the person may cry or say that they will lose their house or apartment.

If these emotions make you queasy, you aren't alone. Firing employees is one of the most difficult parts of owning a business. So what can you do to experience success and lower the likelihood of needing to fire someone?

First, you might want to bring on a new hire as a part-time employee. This protects both of you quite a bit. The employee still has the security of a part-time job, and you have the time to decide if he or she is a good fit. Additionally, you could hire them as a contractor if you need more help but want to avoid payroll tax and fringe benefit liabilities.

Next, the skill set your employee needs to have may be more complex than you might anticipate. First, there are the tasks they will need to complete. Do they have the training, knowledge, or drive to be able to do the work? Of course, for them to do the work, you also need to explain your expectations clearly.

This sounds easy, but there's a reason that business coaches warn employees about the "bring me another rock" employer. This employer asks the employee to complete a task, doesn't give details, then isn't satisfied.

"Bring me a rock."

"What kind of rock?"

"Any kind of rock. I don't care. I just need a rock."

Employee trudges off, gets a rock, and drops it at your feet.

"Oh, I needed a round rock. This is square."

"But you said any rock."

"I know I did, but it really needs to be round. Bring me a round rock."

"Okay, how big?"

"It really doesn't matter. Just normal sized."

Employee trudges off, gets a round rock, and drops it at your feet.

"Oh, it's too small ..."

Don't be that boss. Be clear before your employee sets out to complete a task. You might begin by putting your expectations in writing. This will help you formalize what you want, and the employee has absolute guidance on what to do. Additionally, you both have a document to reference in case the task isn't done to your expectation.

Be careful before you hire family or friends. I know you think you can fire your cousin's niece by marriage, but I'm here to suggest that no, you really can't. It's much easier not to hire someone in the first place than it is to have to fire them later. Or worse, you keep an employee because she is related when she really can't do the job.

I have one last tip when hiring an employee, and it may be the most important one. Remember how we talked about creating your business brand? Your employees will either reinforce your brand or destroy it. They will never be a neutral influence, so it's critical that your employees have the same commitment to your business that you do. Of course, your employees probably don't own any of your business. That's a good thing—at least for a long time. Once you give your employee shares of your business, it's difficult to get it back.

Instead of company ownership to help build loyalty and enthusiasm, provide benefits for your employee that she values. I'm assuming here that you are a small business and are hiring your first employee, or you just have two or three employees. The fewer employees you have, the easier it is to structure benefits in a way that your employees feel valued. These benefits can be the obvious ones—employer-provided insurance, a retirement plan, maybe even a benefits package. However, let's face it. This isn't where you will be starting. At first just making payroll is going to be an accomplishment.

As a result, you may need to get more creative in what benefits you offer. An easy adjustment is to be generous in your leave policy. Yes, you are paying the employees for time they aren't there, but it builds a lot of goodwill. Additionally, I don't know why anyone wants a sick employee to come into the office or store. Other easy benefits are a slightly longer lunch break or paid holidays.

At the end of the day, though, you are looking for an employee whose values line up with yours. Typically, this exists in the employee from the beginning, and then you reinforce it through any benefits you give.

I would make the argument that matching values might be more important than skills. Yes, if a task is highly complex, competence is critical. But many skills can be learned. And your employee is an extension of you.

In summary, don't hire an employee too soon. Be sure you have the funds to make payroll. Be cautious hiring family and friends. And, finally, look for someone with your values. A good employee is the best decision you will ever make, but a bad one can eventually cost you your business. You want to make a good choice!

～

Megan: I try hard to be a good, cheerful employee. After reading this chapter, I need to make sure my boss sees my efforts.

Jessica: We have one co-worker who seems to hate her job. She always takes offense and never participates in company activities. I wonder what she was expecting when she took the job because she doesn't seem happy. I think she'd like us if she took the time to get to know us.

Kim: I don't want to hire any employees for as long as possible. I want to keep the profits for myself, and all I need is software to help me keep a schedule and handle my accounting.

Sharon: I don't understand business owners who think they are too good to do the boring work. They are losing so much potential income. You need to be pretty successful before it makes financial sense to hire someone.

Next Steps

Do you need to hire an employee? Begin by looking at your company brand and goals. When you interview potential hires, ask yourself if the person will be a good fit in your business' culture. Then write a detailed job description that you both use as a reference. Encourage your applicants to define their skills honestly. Remember, if you like the person and you think she or he has a good work ethic, training is relatively easy. Write your notes on the following lines.

Peggy Doviak

. . .

Caring for Parents and Children

Elma Holder: Nursing Home Reformer

Elma Holder graduated from the University of Oklahoma and went to work for the Oklahoma State Health Department in the Medicare survey division. She became concerned with what she noticed around nursing home supervision. The homes seemed to know in advance when survey teams were coming for inspections. The reports also overlooked issues in the facilities.

Unsuccessful in her attempt to reform the system at home, she took a job working for the National Council on Aging in Washington DC. During her three decades in DC, she also worked with Ralph Nader and the Gray Panthers.

In 1975, after attending a nursing home industry conference, Holder co-founded the National Citizens' Coalition for Nursing Home Reform. She served as its executive director for more than twenty-five years.

Two years later, Elma co-authored a book on nursing home conditions. Her tireless efforts led to the passage of the Nursing Home Reform Act of 1987. The Act created both national standards and a bill of rights for nursing home residents offering protection from abuse and a guaranteed level of care.

Even after this major accomplishment, Elma continued to fight for patients' rights. In the 1990s her actions led to a reduction in the use of restraints on confused seniors. She also lobbied for better pay for nursing home workers and improved physical structures.

In 2002, Elma retired and returned home to Oklahoma to care for her own mother, a lucky woman to have such a persistent daughter.

Chapter 22

The Ham in the Sandwich

It was Tuesday. She needed to get the twins to a soccer scrimmage and her daughter to cheerleading practice. Thank God, her girl would be getting her license soon. Her dad had a doctor's appointment, but her mom was going with him and promised to call during the appointment if there were any questions. Sure enough, at five after four, the phone rang. When had those symptoms started again? Her oldest son had just moved back in, needing the free rent since he couldn't find a job in his profession. He was depressed, and it created an odd dynamic in the home as no one knew their role. As soon as everyone was back home, fed, and ready for the next day, she was going to spend a couple of hours working on a presentation she was giving tomorrow. She had been planning to go to yoga today, but she called and cancelled her class. There just wasn't any time.

Do you feel trapped between trying to take care of your kids and helping your parents? Many middle-aged women feel like they are caught in a trap they can't escape. This section of the book looks at what it means to be a caregiver both to your parents and your children.

Raising children is difficult. Don't get me wrong. It's wonderful and rewarding and you wouldn't trade the process (or them) for anything in the world. And eventually they will leave home, ready to take wing! But sometimes they come back. Called "boomerang children," they can't find jobs in their fields that pay sufficient salaries for them to live independently. So they move back in with you. You love them, but you didn't expect this.

Then there are your parents. Slowly, they're aging. Their decline from complete independence begins with more frequent phone calls, then you're going with them to doctor's appointments, and finally helping them in additional, sometimes extensive, ways. You love them enormously, and you will do anything for them. But it takes so much time.

Finally, you have your own financial stability. Whether you are married or single, you have probably included your income in any retirement projections. You can't just quit to find more time. Even if you don't work, then you are busy taking care of children, keeping your own home organized, and providing a caring environment for everyone.

However, now "everyone" is about three times as many people as you were anticipating. You are overwhelmed, stressed out, and don't know what to do. You just keep running.

As a result, this first chapter of the caregiving section isn't about money. Instead, I have tips to help you prosper. Yes, you. First, you deserve it, and second, if you fall apart, this whole house of cards is going to collapse. You need to take care of yourself.

Begin by calling a family meeting to make sure everyone understands what needs to happen. With today's level of college debt and lingering COVID-19 disruptions, many boomerang kids really do need the roof you can provide. But that doesn't mean they can't take an active role in the house to help everything run more smoothly. Meal preparation, lawn care, and cleaning, in addition to any other tasks that require regular attention, should be shared by everyone who lives under the roof. No, your grown kids aren't teenagers, and they won't have a curfew. But if they are responsible adults, they can help.

Younger children can take a role in managing broadened requirements as well. If your parents need additional help and they live close, your teenagers may be able to assist with some tasks, like picking up appropriate prescriptions and buying groceries. The additional time your children are spending with your mom and dad should thrill them, and this may cut down on phone calls that stem from loneliness.

Next, set boundaries for yourself. You do not have to be available to anyone at any hour of the day or night. Of course, emergencies will happen. But often, we borrow trouble long before it appears. Sometimes timeliness is critical, but too often we set deadlines and time horizons on ourselves that aren't expected by the people we are assisting.

Try prioritizing what you have to get done in order to keep yourself competitive at your job. It's important that you thrive at work. I'm assuming you need the money and don't want the trauma of being fired or having to quit. If you are in your fifties and your folks are in their eighties, you could lose your last ten to fifteen years of salary and retirement savings if you leave your job. This can easily lead to personal financial instability and poverty in your own twilight years.

Once your family and work lives are under control, create a plan to keep your personal stress level down and your health and strength optimal. Eat healthy foods, exercise, and get enough sleep. What do you love to do? Build in time to allow yourself to meet your own needs. You can't help others if you fall apart.

The lack of time in the day is one of the most difficult parts of being a caregiver. Look for ways to become more efficient. Each day, review what you need to do for your children and parents. Try to stack events together. For instance, get mom's groceries and yours at the same time. Here's a trick I've used. Tie her bags and leave yours open. That way, when you go to sort them out later, the task will be easier. Make sure your parents have adequate pills in each prescription, so you can pick them up once a month rather than on five different trips. If you have the financial resources, hire a housekeeper to help them out a couple of times a month. You may find that more useful than having someone clean your own house.

As another strategy, take some shortcuts. Paper plates are fine, especially if they are filled with an easy to prepare homemade crockpot meal that you can serve a couple of times. And your house may not be dust free, although you might know a thirteen-year-old who would be happy to fix that for a nominal fee. You have to take care of yourself. No one wants you to be struggling. If it feels that way, it's likely a result of others simply not thinking what they are asking of you. It's difficult, but it's up to you to share your feelings with them.

There isn't one solution to feeling like the ham in the sandwich. Countless articles are written about it regularly, and the phenomenon is driving middle-aged women crazy. It's hard to breathe, let alone prosper, when you feel trapped. But a little organization will go a long way. And don't feel ashamed to ask the people in your life to take on some extra responsibility.

The remaining chapters in this section give you strategies

for other specific issues you may be facing. Just remember you aren't alone.

Megan: Fortunately, my mom is still healthy, but I feel overwhelmed just taking care of Charlotte. I can't imagine worrying about her too.

Jessica: I was lucky to find a job in my field, but my little brother is still at home. He can't find a job in his major. I'm going to suggest that he pitch in a little more to make mom's life easier.

Kim: I know so many women a little older than I am who I think are losing their minds trying to juggle everything. It's important that they don't lose themselves as they are taking care of everyone else.

Sharon: Pressures today are overwhelming, and it seems like we are going at a faster pace. I'm glad that my kids are settled, finally, with real jobs. I don't need their assistance, which helps, because their kids go in a thousand directions at once. When I do need them, I hope I can remember to be generous with my schedule.

Next Steps

It's okay to admit you need some assistance. If you feel like you are being pressured on all sides, call a family meeting. If you can include your parents, great. If that's not feasible, then at least create a plan within your core family. Divide tasks like cooking, cleaning, and running errands. If everyone does a little, no one will have to do a lot. Choose three chores you can delegate, and write them on the following lines. In the meeting, you can create additional strategies.

Chapter 23

Medicare and Medicaid

The websites were confusing, and the Medicare supplement insurance salesperson talked so fast. More than anything, Mom didn't want to go into a nursing home, but if she did have to move, she would need some financial assistance. She thought either Medicare or her supplement covered nursing home costs. When she read in a senior magazine that she didn't have the long-term care coverage she thought, she panicked. What could she do?

I'm concerned that many people misunderstand Medicare and Medicaid benefits, especially when it comes to paying for long-term care. Rather than offering a reliable source of funding, Medicare's long-term care coverage is extremely restricted, and Medicaid is either inaccessible or available only with drawbacks that might be unexpected. Before you make inaccurate assumptions there are a few things about Medicare and Medicaid I want you to understand.

First, let's look at the different characteristics. Medicare is healthcare for the elderly or disabled, while Medicaid is healthcare for the indigent. If you are sixty-five or older, you likely have Medicare benefits. Medicare is divided primarily into Parts A, B, and D. Medicare A covers hospitalization, skilled nursing facility care, home healthcare services, and hospice.

"Wait a minute!" you say. "You just told me that Medicare wasn't a good provider of long-term care, but it's listed right there—skilled nursing facility care—under the components of Part A."

Yes, there are some long-term care benefits to Medicare. However, a hospital stay must occur prior to qualifying for skilled nursing facility care. Even then, the care phases out and is gone after 101 days. Also, notice that the coverage is for skilled nursing. Most people requiring long-term care don't need skilled nursing; they need custodial care, which isn't covered. And they need it for longer than 101 days. For most people, Medicare won't provide a usable and sufficient benefit for late life care.

Medicaid, on the other hand, is healthcare coverage for low-income adults and children. Many people who would never consider using Medicaid as their primary insurance (even if they could), plan to use it to pay for their long-term care. This is difficult for many reasons.

First, to rely on Medicaid for your long-term care funding, you must have virtually no financial resources. To reach this point, you have to spend almost everything you own before you qualify to use the service. In the past, some people found a way around this. They just gave their assets to their children, and surprise—they were broke.

The Medicaid system got wise to that strategy and originally created a three-year lookback period. Even this restriction wasn't sufficient, and Medicaid extended their requirements. Now it's a five-year window. Any assets that are given away during this five-year period count as current assets.

The nursing home must be paid out of the pocket of the potential Medicaid recipient before Medicaid begins to pay. For example, assume the senior gives fifty thousand dollars to her grandchildren less than five years from requesting Medicaid benefits. She must pay fifty thousand to the nursing home before Medicaid will pick up the bill. Additionally, you need to be careful how you structure a spend down even more than five years back.

You may have one option to protect some of your assets, a "Medicaid Trust." You should talk to an attorney to review the details and see if the structure would work for you. Medicaid fraud is a prosecutable offense, and the rules about the legality of Medicaid planning are ever changing.

After all these rules, it's still not easy. Assume your mom needs care, and she financially qualifies for a Medicaid bed. You could still have trouble. Because end of life care is so expensive, Medicaid beds go fast. They don't exist in every nursing home, and probably that country club-like facility you want isn't going to offer a Medicaid bed at all. Even in facilities that offer them, the number of available beds is low. You may have a long wait until your mother can get a room.

When you are faced with a care emergency, you usually don't have the option to wait. As a result, you may find you have to place your mother in a home thirty or forty miles or farther from where you live. This will make visiting and checking on her condition difficult.

Then there's the level of care. You may be surprised that I am not going to be as critical of this as you would expect. We all read about the awful abuse and neglect in some nursing homes. People who abuse the elderly are the lowest of the low. However, often employees do the best they can.

The biggest care issue in Medicaid nursing facilities involves the number of patients and limited resources. The

Medicaid system often doesn't have adequate funding to complete the job they've been given. When a caregiver is responsible for a significant number of dementia patients, keeping up with all of them can be a challenge, if not impossible. The burnout rate for care providers is high, and the number of seniors keeps increasing. It's all the ingredients for a disaster.

Using Medicaid resources is more than appropriate if you qualify for them, and sometimes there are no options. I just want to be sure you understand that Medicare is not a good long-term solution for most elder care, and Medicaid can be more troubling than you anticipated. As a result, you may want to try to find some additional funding for your parents' care. We'll look at those strategies in the next chapter.

Megan: Of course, most of this chapter assumes people have resources. Sometimes, qualifying for Medicaid isn't difficult at all.

Jessica: I wonder if Medicare will even be around when I'm sixty-five. I hope so.

Kim: Sam's mother doesn't have a lot of money, and we're doing okay, but not good enough to be able to pay her expenses. I'm hoping that we can plan in advance to use a Medicaid facility close to where we live. I just don't see another way.

Sharon: So many of my friends don't understand Medicare benefits. I don't think the government meant to make it confusing, but it is. We all need to take the time to see what we do and don't have.

Next Steps

If your parents qualify for Medicaid, and you want to use the benefit, then start planning early to try to access a facility close to your home. If not, then you may want to look at other financial solutions to meet their long-term care needs. Jot your notes on the following lines.

_____

_____

_____

_____

_____

_____

_____

Chapter 24

Long-Term Care

It was different a hundred years ago. Parents either already lived with adult children, or they moved there when they started having difficulties. Between larger families with more children, fewer women working, and a shorter life expectancy, it was relatively easy to care for grandma or grandpa. Today, many people live into their nineties, often dying from dementia-related illness, making family care almost impossible. Additionally, our mobile society creates long distances between parents and children. It's easier to check on mom when she lives around the corner. We have smaller families, and the children are busy with scheduled activities. And still. . .your surviving parent (probably your mother) needs care. The only option for many is to pay for it.

As WE LEARNED in the last chapter, Medicare and Medicaid may not provide the financial resources to pay for the last years of your life or your parents' lives. I think the cost of this care can be one of the most challenging financial planning issues. It's common for a nursing home, memory care unit, or home care company to charge six, seven, or even eight thousand dollars A MONTH. And most people spend about three years in this situation. At that rate, it can require that you have $250,000 saved and invested to be fairly certain you will have enough money. What do you do? Fortunately, you have some options that we will look at in this chapter.

Before we get into the cost of care too deeply, a word of caution. I've seen grown children keen to move their parents into some kind of senior living long before they need it or are ready. Additionally, I suggest you not continually pressure them into moving into your home. People are living vibrant lives well into their eighties, and it's possible that they don't want to live with you yet. When things go well, both the parents and the children recognize when it's safe for the senior to live alone and when further steps need to be taken. Unfortunately, I've also seen times when a parent was unwilling to recognize an unsafe situation. I've also experienced overly protective children who can't believe their parents can find their way home because they are seventy! Listen to each other, and possibly everyone will need to compromise a little. Hopefully, the safe decisions can be made in a way that no one finds objectionable.

Still, there will come a time when mom can't live alone. Further, most people haven't saved enough to be able to pay for their retirement and have a quarter million dollars left over for caregiving expenses! If you find your parents in that situation, don't be ashamed. For many years I've said that end of life care is the planning monster no one wants to talk about, because it is impossibly daunting. Fortunately, there are a few things you can do to make it less scary. The first is to consider your options.

Move Mom into Your Home

Maybe when it's time, you, or one of your siblings, will consider moving mom into your home—or theirs. Be warned—this option sometimes looks better in movies than it does in real life. Having a senior citizen move into the home can put a strain on everyone. Before you even consider it, talk to your spouse and children, and discuss the impact such a move could have on the family. Which room would become mom's? Which bathroom would she use? How will her presence affect sleep schedules? The need for quiet after her bedtime? On the positive side, having a grandparent living under the roof might provide some free babysitting if they are still vibrant but unsure about living alone. Living with older family members can also teach children about their heritage, the experiences of their grandparents when they were young, and simple empathy for other human beings.

However, moving a parent into your home isn't always the best option. First, if the parent requires constant care, you will likely have to hire an agency or a private duty aide to be with your mom when you are all at work. Having a stranger living in your home is okay for some people, but it doesn't work for everyone.

If you're thinking you'll take care of your mother yourself, just know that sometimes this is a great strategy, and sometimes it's catastrophic. First, if you already work, your family finances probably can't survive the loss of income your job provides. Your mom won't be living there forever. Even if you can survive a period without your current income, what will you do when you're alone again? Ending your career to take care of your parents yourself is likely a bad idea. And it can get worse. When a parent develops dementia, she often feels like people are stealing from her or trying to harm her. This creates an impossible situation in your home and may force you to consider other options.

Keep Mom in her Home

If you don't want to use a facility, you could have your mother remain in her own home and use an agency or private duty nurse to stay with her there. If you can afford it, this has many advantages. First, if your mom has dementia, you won't have to put her through the trauma of moving her into an unknown facility. Changes of venue can be stressful for dementia patients. Keeping your mom in her home also helps ensure that she gets personalized care. And if there is another disease outbreak, she may be less likely to contract it outside of a group setting. Of course, the crisis here is the high cost of this option. As part of a meeting with your siblings and your parents, you will need to establish a care plan.

Move Mom into a Facility

You may start by keeping your mom at home and move her to a facility later if your resources can't continue to cover the steep home caregiving. Unfortunately, if your mother has dementia, moving her when her disease has advanced is likely to lead to a fairly significant decline. If she gets used to her new surroundings while she is still more aware, the transition is likely to be much easier for her.

Continuing in this mode, there are multiple kinds of facilities from which you can choose. Even though the Veterans Administration is often in the media with issues, many VA nursing homes are quite nice. If either of your parents is eligible, you might want to visit the local facility, as the amount owed can be based on their ability to pay.

Opt for a Retirement Center or "Aging in Place" Facility

Additionally, you may select from retirement centers that offer almost independent living. Retirement centers have many amenities and may even allow "aging in place." This structure allows the parent to transition among different levels of care. Other retirement centers have minimum ability requirements, so it's important to look at what services are available.

Select a Skilled Memory Care or Nursing Facility

You might also consider a memory care facility for those suffering with dementia. Finally, nursing homes offer advanced care.

Whatever you choose, I recommend that you visit any facilities you are considering at various times of day and without calling in advance. Additionally, I would continue to drop by their home or facility once your parents are living there. You want to know what goes on when the caregiver doesn't think anyone is watching.

You can put together a great care plan, but you'll still need to pay the bill. One option is to use your parents' home as a resource. Outside of selling it, two other options are reverse mortgages and lines of credit.

Reverse mortgages provide funds that do not need to be repaid, and nearly always (but read the fine print), your parents can remain in their home as long as they wish. However, reverse mortgages may not provide as much access to equity as you expect, and they can have high fees. Further, once the second parent leaves the house, it belongs to the lending agency who will sell it to get their money back and give you anything that remains. You probably shouldn't count on much because they likely won't seek top dollar.

I'm not as opposed to reverse mortgages as some articles I have read. However, I will admit to being slightly suspicious of products being sold by washed-up actors on high-number television channels at three in the morning. These studs of yesteryear stand in front of luxury automobiles parked in front of mansions. They explain that you, too, can experience financial security if you just take out a reverse mortgage. Taking a reverse mortgage for these reasons makes me crazy. I believe they are a planning strategy of last resort. Reverse mortgages should be used to allow people to stay in their homes and avoid a Medicaid facility—not to fund a lavish early retirement.

Creating a line of credit against the home's equity might be a better option than a reverse mortgage. However, its effectiveness will depend on whether you and your siblings have both the resources and desire to make the loan payments. With a line of credit, money is only borrowed as it is needed, and then it is paid back in monthly installments. If you and your siblings could pay that note, you would retain complete control over the asset. Once something happens to your parents, then you get to decide whether to sell the house or keep it and continue making payments.

Simplest, perhaps, is selling the home outright if your parent or parents are going into a nursing home or retirement center. That way, the assets are available to help make the payments. The biggest drawback to this idea is that most people want to stay in their homes. Of course, that makes selling the home not an option.

Long Term Care Insurance

Long-term care insurance provides funds that can be used to cover housing and caregiving options. I know the product gets a lot of grief, and some is deserved. Qualifying for the policy is difficult, and boy, is it expensive! Many people look at the cost of the premium and say, "I'll just take my chances."

You can choose that option, as well; however, you should make your decision from an informed position. Realize that one of the reasons for the cost is that long-term care is just barely an insurable condition. Remember how insurance works. You purchase homeowners' insurance from the fear that something catastrophic will happen to your home. You're afraid of fire, tornadoes, theft, damage, and many other things. And you are wise to carry good coverage. Your house is probably your biggest asset, and if you lost it without insurance, it would be a disaster.

The insurance company knows, however, that it will take in far more premium than it will pay on claims. Most people's homes will not suffer catastrophic loss.

This concept is called "the law of large numbers," and it's vital for insurance to be successful. Insurance works because most of us won't claim as much as we pay. Now, think again about long-term care insurance.

It's great that we have discovered cures for so many diseases and conditions. No one wants to go back to the time when people died young, and we all do everything in our power to extend our lives. Statistics suggest that for people my age—fifty-ish—we will probably die from situations related to dementia. It will be the leading cause of death.

Dementia is also one of the primary reasons people use long-term care. If most of us are going to have dementia late in life, then we will be using the long-term care insurance we purchased. This defies the concept of insurance.

Insurance companies have dealt with this reality in a number of ways. Some companies no longer sell long-term care policies. The companies that do sell policies have been forced to raise premium costs. Additionally, they send incentives designed to lower their risk by offering policy holders lower premiums if they drop inflation protection, cap benefits, or shorten coverage periods. Remember, when offers seem good, they may not be in your best interest. If you get such an offer, examine it carefully before you choose what you will do.

A relatively new change in the long-term care market is the invention of new products that offer far less long-term coverage in conjunction with life insurance. Of course, you need to talk to your CFP® pro along with the insurance specialist, if you are working with two people, before you decide if these hybrid plans are for you, but I would offer a little advice. Be certain that the coverage you are purchasing is the coverage you need. This kind of hybrid product focuses on the addition of a death benefit for your family, but did you really need more life insurance? Does the long-term care offered provide you with enough benefit? Of course, if you don't qualify for traditional long-term care insurance, then your options are limited, and the hybrid plan might be more appealing. Just always understand what you are purchasing. You want to be sure that you are gaining more financial advantage from purchasing the policy than you would by simply saving the money and paying for your own care.

If you look at the appropriateness of these plans, the answer might be quite different for you and your mother. If your mother qualified for a hybrid plan, the benefit would be in place much earlier than if she tried to save the money. On the other side, you may still have years left to fund your own long-term care. This is why so little financial planning involves one correct answer. Your circumstances are everything. Look at your long-term care needs and your parents' long-term care needs and make the decisions that will keep everyone in a good place.

Finally, less traditional care models are beginning to emerge as at least partial solutions to the long-term care crisis. Remember the television show, *The Golden Girls*? People are opting to live with friends, and this companionship and shared duties can allow independent living for many years. Additionally, communities with small homes are being developed where seniors live alone but in proximity to others. Cooking is communal, and meals are shared. I believe these solutions are just the tip of the iceberg of things to come. Look at all your long-term care options, and don't take the first idea you see. There might be a better way.

Megan: My grandmother has Alzheimer's. It's a horrible disease.

Jessica: I hope medicine finds a cure for dementia before I'm older.

Kim: Sam needs to look at some of these co-housing options for her mom. She has lots of friends, and I think they would rather live together than in a stuffy senior home.

> Sharon: I was shocked when my friend Ruth had to move out of her retirement center when she started falling. Just when she needed the friends she had made, she was forced into a new facility where she didn't know anyone.

Next Steps

You will probably have the most success if you combine two or three of the ideas in this chapter. Call a family meeting and create a care plan for your parents. Then jot your notes on the following lines.

Chapter 25

Your Parents' Estate Plan

She was smart, proud, and a professional. She didn't want her children to know much about her money because she thought it wasn't any of their business. She told the professionals in her life—her accountant, attorney, and financial planner—they weren't to share her information with anyone. And her mind was sound, so all they could do was try to convince her otherwise. Then her mind began to slip, and her children approached the professionals to try to assist their mom. With no documents in place, they had to create a court-ordered guardianship. It was painful and embarrassing to them, but they didn't have any options.

No ONE WANTS to think about their end of life. We all believe we will live forever, and we want to be strong and independent. However, aging happens to all of us. One of the hardest tasks is talking to your parents about aging issues. It's even more difficult than facing your own mortality. However, the more of an estate plan you can help your parents make in advance, the easier everything will be down the road.

So how do you bring up the topic? You are probably in a

better position to make that decision than I am. You want to try to choose a time that isn't tied to a crisis. Maybe you take them out to lunch or invite them over for coffee and dessert—or maybe even a good, stiff drink!

Parents usually want to help their children. If you can help your parents see that creating an estate plan will make your life and the lives of your siblings easier, the discussion will more likely go better. And it may need to be a series of talks rather than one giant, depressing conversation. But over time there are some issues you want to resolve.

First, your parents need a power of attorney for healthcare and a power of attorney for finance. Many attorneys draw these up as one document, but remember that different people can hold the powers. Of course, spouses usually count on their partners as their first line of defense, but it's important that there also be younger family members involved.

Family dynamics can come into play in these situations. Mom and dad may have strong feelings about who they want to hold their powers of attorney. Once they have their ideas finalized but before the documents are created, call a family meeting, so everyone knows what's going on. Never appoint a power of attorney to someone who doesn't know they hold it or who doesn't agree to the responsibility!

A family meeting about your parents' estate can be an uncomfortable conversation. It's common for one or more siblings not to want to deal with their parents' aging. Unfortunately, you need to have the conversation anyway.

If there seem to be hard feelings, with a sibling feeling slighted, remember that powers of attorney can be held jointly, with majority rule in case of disagreement. This lets everyone work together on making decisions, especially those around healthcare.

Another document, an advanced directive, or "living

will," can also help lower future stress for you and your siblings. Advanced directives aren't moral documents, even though they are sometimes portrayed that way. All they provide is a guideline for the type of care the creator wants. If your parents want care like hydration, nutrition, or a ventilator, this is the document that guarantees they will get it. On the other hand, if they don't want those or similar treatments, the document keeps the children from having to make horrendous decisions. Not having an advanced directive can be catastrophic, especially if your parents are on a trip and something goes very wrong hundreds of miles away from the medical community that knows them. In a world after COVID, you need to have a gentle but in-depth conversation about the treatments your parents want. The choices of recent years were heartbreaking, and they put living will issues in a different light than they had before 2020.

Both powers of attorney and living wills concern diminished capacity and end-of-life issues, but other documents are still needed to be sure your parents' wishes are followed after they have passed. The division of estate assets can be complicated, and it's important that your parents have at least a will and possibly a trust to make sure the assets are divided in the way they desire.

Remember that having only a will likely subjects at least part of the estate to probate—the court process ensuring that debts are paid, and assets go to the correct beneficiaries. Items avoid probate when they are held in survivorship ownership, passed through beneficiary, or are divided in a trust. The death of the first parent may not create a major crisis, assuming that assets are held jointly. Even in community property states, there are some ways of creating survivorship. However, the death of the second parent is where probate is likely to become an issue. It's important for you and your parents to meet with an estate attorney in your state to see what titling options are available.

Additionally, the attorney can help draw up other documents that your parents might need, so the assets can pass according to their wishes. Using online services may not provide the level of detail needed in the estate. Worse yet, the documents available online might not be recognized in your state. Working with a good estate attorney can avoid problems you don't even know exist.

Before the final documents are created, you may want to have a second family meeting to discuss which individual items each member wants so your folks can provide for these in their will and/or trust. I've seen people take this to the level where names were written on the bottom of items.

That might be a little too much planning, even for me! However, if it works for your family, that's great. Otherwise, the family can decide those details in the future.

Your parents have control of their estate until the day they die. Anticipating inherited assets is no excuse for failing to create your own financial plan. Health issues and life changes may deplete your parents' resources. If an inheritance is your retirement plan and the money is spent, then you will become a burden to your children. I'm sure you don't want that.

The final piece of the written estate plan is easy, but it's often overlooked. Your parents need to make a list of where everything is located. Where are the brokerage statements, insurance policies, titles, deeds, patents, bank boxes, and mineral rights? Who is the financial adviser, insurance agent, CPA, and attorney? Finally, what are the passwords to the online information? When I talk to clients about putting together a list, some of them already have them. When I ask them if their spouse knows the password to their computer, they look at me in horror. I've never had anyone say yes. We have passwords for our passwords these days, and they will need to be updated regularly. If that is too much of a hassle in day-to-day life, at least have your parents write down their online services, the latest password, and today's date on a sheet of paper and put it in the folder. Even if the password is out of date, the family will know that there is an account or document located there, and they will be able to run it down eventually.

Your parents' list of assets can exist online, but it also needs to be written down on paper. Then, someone, or preferably several people, either need a copy or at least knowledge of where the list is located. Some parents don't feel comfortable sharing their entire financial lives with their children. That's okay—they don't have to. They might just tell them where the list can be found.

Although thinking about your parents' estate can be unpleasant for both of you, it's an important series of conversations and tasks. If you have no success when you mention it the first time, bring it up periodically. Additionally, if you hear stories of estate disasters, you might share them to encourage your parents to take action. I have found that otherwise organized clients avoid creating estate plans. However, it's tremendously important. Maybe if you tell your parents that you are creating your estate plan, you might motivate them also. Then both of you have completed an important part of your family's financial security!

Megan: My mom's so young I'm not sure I want to talk to her about her estate plan yet.

Jessica: Before I try to talk to my folks about having estate documents in place, I better do it myself! I'm especially worried about having a medical power of attorney and an advanced directive.

Kim: If Sam and I were married, our estate plan would be a lot easier. As it is, we don't have any of the spousal assumptions of inheriting assets. We've had an estate plan in place for years, and we've both talked to our folks. I'm glad they're all reasonable and willing to deal with unpleasant topics.

Sharon: We had probate issues when my mother died. She didn't do anything after my dad passed away, and it caused a real problem with the house and her two cars.

Next Steps

Maybe the best way to begin a conversation about estate planning with your parents is by discussing your own documents. If you don't have an estate plan yet, put one in place. This will also give you an opportunity to interview lawyers. Try to select one that can also help your folks, as this continuity will make your life much easier. You might want to consider someone who specializes in eldercare. Jot your ideas on the following lines.

Chapter 26

Teaching Children about Money

When she was young, no one in her family talked about money. Even when her father was laid off, he never discussed finances. Now she had children of her own, and she wanted to help them not make the mistakes of her past. But she didn't know how to talk to them about money.

WE WANT to keep our children safe. We teach them not to talk to strangers and to eat their broccoli. We tell them to brush their teeth and not to smoke. We encourage them to be respectful, hardworking, honest, and kind. But we don't teach them about money.

For many of us "of a certain age," money wasn't talked about in the home. It was considered rude and inappropriate. But those days are gone. Now we talk about almost everything. Ads on television cover subjects that are incredibly embarrassing and impossible to explain during dinner. People go on talk shows and confess to just about anything. But we still don't talk about money.

Think about what you discuss with your friends. Do they know your bills? Do you even talk about expenses with your spouse (without fighting)? Do you shelter your children from all references to money? By keeping your children financially in the dark, you are doing them no favor.

Of course, the discussion is complex. Children are powerless, and they have no way to make money. As a result, it's absolutely unfair to burden them with major financial difficulties. However, teaching your children healthy relationships with money gives them tools they are unlikely to learn anywhere else. Different activities and levels of information at the appropriate ages will help them enormously.

You might be surprised to learn that you can begin to teach your children about money by the time you are reading stories to them. There are many good children's books that teach useful financial lessons. You and your children should plan a trip to the library or bookstore and choose something you both find interesting.

Once your kids get a little older, give them an allowance and use it as a tool to teach them about money. I think it's useful for them to see how work and money are related. If you want to give them a base allowance amount, that's fine. But then I like the idea of giving them an opportunity to earn additional money for completing tasks.

Earning money can teach your children responsibility and will help them begin to see why most adults have a career. I've heard the criticism that children should do tasks because they are members of the household. I totally understand that; however, most of us work for money. Children don't have the ability to leave the house and go to work. If we are going to help them understand the purpose of work in the "real world," it helps to provide them with a similar environment.

As you structure how your children will receive money, be sure to consult your spouse or partner. You should present a united financial front to your kids, so it doesn't matter which parent the child approaches with a financial request. Both of you should give the same answer.

Unfortunately, providing a united front can get complicated. If you are divorced and share custody with your spouse, financial behaviors often become central, especially when one of the parents has more money. If you are the parent with the higher salary, you should not try to buy your child's affection with great gifts that you know your ex-spouse can't afford. However, it's much more difficult when you are the spouse with fewer resources, and you can't afford to give gifts on the level your ex is providing.

Financial one-upmanship is a tricky situation to manage. And it can hurt when your children come home with the expensive gifts you know they want. Don't feel bad. Your children won't even think to tell you how much they value the time you are giving them. Do not create debt trying to keep up with your ex, even if his behavior is driving you crazy.

It's useful to show your children how working allows them to purchase items they want. However, I think it's also good to encourage them to be generous with money. Let them put change in the buckets outside the malls around the holidays. If you go to a house of worship, give them a little money to donate.

When your children are young, don't overly explain how they are giving to help certain causes or people who are in need. That's a complicated concept for a young child, and it might raise anxieties that they don't even express to you. However, as they get older, it's important for them to understand why you have taught them to be generous. They should have a good understanding of the real world by the time they are in high school. You might think older teens understand the world, but high school kids can be insulated in their immediate circle of friends. As a result, they will tend to see the world in only those terms. If their peers are activists or humanitarians, they may have a keen understanding. However, if the focus is on the next dance or game (not bad places for them to focus), you may have to teach them how to be generous. You can also remind them at this age that generosity is not just money. Gifts of time can be even more useful.

Regarding charity, I also believe that it's important for children not just to receive gifts on holidays and for birthdays. When they are in early grade school, let them help you pick out a gift for them to give, put their name on it, and let the gift come from them. Your own financial situation will determine where you shop for this gift. However, as they get older, encourage them to use their allowance to purchase gifts for family members. If you want, you could bump up the allowance a little around holidays. Or better than that, teach them to budget throughout the year. Make giving the gift an exciting event for them, not something that they do only because they have to do it.

The point of this is not to get your children to buy you something. Instead, I think that financial responsibility involves being an equal partner in financial situations rather than simply receiving things. I believe that children should not think that the world exists simply to serve their needs. I know some of you will not want to do this. But having your children purchase a thoughtful gift at the dollar store for their sibling is a good lesson. And when they can tell that sibling that they actually paid for the gift, themselves, it gives them a sense of financial independence.

As your children get older and want certain items, there is nothing wrong with explaining to them how much you will have to work to provide it. Now, I'm not suggesting that you do this with the monthly bills that have to be paid—only the special things they want. If you don't want to put it in the frame of your salary, then explain it in terms of a bill they may understand more easily. For example, you could show them how many weeks they would need to save their allowance to have that much.

Children have absolutely no concept of money. Let's face it; many adults don't either. Money is vague and abstract. We have to provide a frame of reference for them and make it real. Begin the lessons when they are young, and let them evolve as your children get older. As their tastes get expensive, your ability to contextualize their spending will improve, as well.

Another great place to teach children to budget is in advance of family trips. Encourage your child to save part of their allowance, so they can have spending money. Since the trip is likely several months away, they will have time to see the value of saving small amounts repeatedly. Of course, they won't be paying the major expenses. However, they could use the money they saved for the incidental purchases.

If this seems too complex, then you and your partner can decide how much spending money you want them to have. Then, give your children a lump sum at the beginning of the trip and tell them how many days it needs to last. For example, I wouldn't recommend handing a ten-year-old a lump sum amount for a two-week trip. You might give them the money you think would be appropriate for two or three days. Once you give it, you tell them that this is for the purchases they want. But they won't get any more until the date reaches your predetermined time. On the flip side, tell them that they get to keep any money they don't spend. If they spend it all at the first gas station, you let them do it. But then, they don't get any more money for the next two days! You may be surprised, however. Your child who would beg you for something every time the vehicle slows down may become a miser and consume absolutely no snacks for two straight days.

Once children are in high school, you should begin to explain budgeting and credit cards to them. This builds easily from the vacation and holiday savings you are already encouraging. But by high school it's important that teens understand the cost of their cell phone, car payments, car insurance, and other costs that impact them, even though they are not yet paying the bills. You want them to have a realistic concept of the cost of living as they prepare to live on their own. And at this point it's fine to share with them that sometimes there are purchases you would like to make but can't afford. Help your teens build a realistic perspective of money.

Additionally, you should warn your teens about the impact of credit card balances. Yes, it's fine to use a card, but you should teach your teens to pay the card off each month. If you are currently carrying a card balance, this is a wonderful time to create a plan to pay off your debt. You don't need to share all your financial information with your teens, but teaching them good habits may inspire you as well!

At some point, your teen or college student may want to begin to build credit. Of course, a credit card is a reasonable way to do this. Unfortunately, the easiest cards to get are often at the mall in stores that only sell discretionary purchases that they might want but don't need.

Instead, consider helping your teen apply for a gas card where they regularly purchase fuel for their vehicle. The advantage of a gas card is that discretionary purchases are limited to the convenience store items found inside. The ability to get in massive credit card debt in a gas station mini mart just isn't high. Additionally, they will be purchasing the gas anyway. They can build credit while they are not spending any more money than they would in the first place.

Once your children have gone to college or are living on their own, continue to talk about money. Encourage them to create a budget using a phone app, even if the balance is pretty close to zero at the end of each month. If they have any money left at all, try to help them start saving their own emergency fund.

Most of all, be a good example. It's fine for your children to see that the family lives on a budget. Once they are teens, it's okay for them to have a basic sense of the bills. You can actually share that with them if you are uncomfortable telling them your salary. We'll talk about how to accomplish this in the next chapter. Your life is more effective than the longest lecture.

Megan: Charlotte's a little young still, but I plan to begin by reading her books that explain money to children. There are a few of them out there.

Jessica: My sister encourages her kids to give a little money to charity. She doesn't want them to grow up selfish.

Kim: I'm surprised how little the schools teach kids about life skills they will need to survive.

Sharon: When I was young, we never talked to our kids about what we could and couldn't afford. I'm so glad they are more honest with their children.

Next Steps

What kind of activities could you use with the children in your life to teach them about money? Jot your ideas on the following lines.

Chapter 27

Your Financial Life and Your Children

She worked longer hours than she wanted and couldn't always spend as much time with her daughter as they both hoped. Limited finances were the results of a divorce five years ago. She never spoke badly of her husband, but she knew the girl recognized the financial change. One day, she decided to share some of the bills with her—after all, her daughter was fifteen. The girl looked at the rent and car payment bills with wide eyes, and she realized how hard her mother had to work. The mother explained that there couldn't be a car next year for the teen's sixteenth birthday. However, she showed her that at her current savings rate, she could probably get the girl in wheels by the time she was seventeen. Her daughter was a little disappointed at first, as you'd expect, but told her mom how glad she was to know the truth.

IN THE LAST CHAPTER, we looked at ways of teaching your children about money, and I ended the chapter suggesting that it's okay for you to share some of your personal financial information with your children. Before we go any further into this topic, I want to offer some advice and a word of caution.

Children are smarter and more observant than we often give them credit. If your family is having severe financial hardship, don't share all of this with your children. They aren't in a position to be able to help you, and all you will do is frighten them. It's okay to be realistic, but sometimes I've seen parents talk to their children like they are their best friends and equals. Because they are minors, children have significantly less power and control than parents do. Being honest is fine. Putting your children under tremendous stress is not.

However, oversharing financial difficulties is not the common tactic taken by parents. More often, they want to keep their finances a complete secret from their children. Even worse, sometimes they want their children to think they have more money than they have. This can end in disaster for everyone.

On the other hand, sharing healthy money behaviors and beliefs with your children can set them up for a lifetime of good personal financial decisions. When children watch you live within your means, save money, and reduce debt, they are more likely to value those characteristics.

For example, when children are young, it's fine to let them know that the spending limits you gave them are not because you are "mean." You can let them know that your home is financially stable, but that money isn't unlimited. As they get older and their taste in gifts gets more expensive, you might encourage them to prioritize what they want the most. They also don't need a new car when they turn sixteen, even though they might think they do!

As a parent, making financial decisions about our children can be painful. We want our children happy, and unfortunately, in today's world, happiness and money are inextricably linked. Our kids may honestly believe that material goods are the source of happiness. It's up to us to convince them that they aren't. It's a huge challenge, but it's tremendously important.

Of course, the way you and your partner respond to money will reinforce your words or negate them. If you convey (or actually hold) a belief that money buys happiness, it won't matter what you say to your child. As adults, we can easily fall into the trap of viewing our own success through our possessions. And yet, what matters most often can't be purchased. If we lose sight of that, conflict is almost inevitable.

Kids are smart and they know when you and your partner aren't getting along. But don't fight about money in front of them. Avoid sarcastic statements about how much your spouse spends or wastes. This bickering back and forth creates a tension of winners and losers and teaches your child that money is stressful. It might also teach them to hide spending, lie about money, or binge spend when they are upset. They are watching you.

With this in mind, you and your partner should talk to your children about how you saved an emergency fund or participated in your 401(k) plan at work. You might talk to them about the investments you chose and why you believe your choices will help you meet your financial goals. You can talk to them about your taxes and the kinds of documents you need to assemble to complete the forms or turn them over to your CPA.

You can have all these conversations with or without sharing the specific numbers with them. If you do share the data, you should contextualize your income with your bills. When your teens see a pay stub, it may seem unbelievably huge. Show them how quickly it disappears in your mortgage or rent, car payment, utilities, and other bills. This gives them a healthy perspective on earning and responsibility.

Of course, talking about money shouldn't be a major topic

with your children. However, if you incorporate honest financial dialogue in organic ways, they will come to view healthy financial practices as typical behaviors.

> Megan: I want to raise Charlotte to be good with money. I think being pretty honest with her will help. Her dad seems to have more money than I do, so I will need to explain it somehow as she gets older.

> Jessica: My mom has done a good job helping me understand money since I was a teenager. She never scared me, but I knew we didn't have enough money for me to have everything I wanted.

> Kim: My dad wanted us to think he was wealthy. He was always spending money, and it wasn't until years later I figured out that he didn't have it. All my childhood memories about money involve lies. I decided I would never be that way.

> Sharon: When I was young, my parents never talked about money. Once I was grown, I realized I had no idea how the financial world worked. I wasn't even comfortable writing checks.

Next Steps

You and your partner should talk about how you want to approach financial conversations with your children. If your partner is opposed to the idea, encourage him or her to read this chapter! If you can get on the same page about this topic, you may find that it lowers the stress in your conversations about money. Jot your ideas on the following lines.

Chapter 28

College for You and Your Kids

She married her high school sweetheart right after graduation. Before long, there was a baby and then another. She had always wanted to be a science teacher, but college seemed unattainable. Now, with kids in high school looking to attend college in just a few years, she wondered if there was a way to accomplish her goal.

I HAVE READ several articles recently about why a college degree isn't important and how we should be focusing attention on mentorships, internships, and trade certifications. Certainly, I understand that college isn't for everyone; however, many careers require formal training. Lacking a college degree creates a barrier of entry to many professions, especially those that have high earning capacities.

With all your responsibilities, how do you find time to earn a college degree on top of everything else you're trying to do? And maybe more importantly, how do you pay for it? Some of the strategies you can use to pay for your own education are similar to ways you help fund your children's schooling, and some are quite different.

A common college funding tool, the 529 plan, is probably more effective for funding your children's education than it is useful for you. 529 plans are funded in after-tax dollars, don't have an income phaseout, and allow large contributions. However, the greatest advantage of the 529 is the tax-free investment gain when the money is used for approved educational expenses. A long time horizon is required to achieve those gains. Children typically have this time before they enter college. However, you may not want to wait fifteen years to start your education! You will need other strategies.

Remember, if you have money in the 529 plan that isn't needed for your child's education, you can use those funds for your own education. Also, immediate family members of 529 beneficiaries can use the funds to pay for their own education. Additionally, recent legislation allows unused 529 funds to be rolled into a Roth IRA for the benefit of the child. The ability to transfer the benefits alleviate the fear of funding a 529 plan for a young child. At that age, you don't know if they will earn a full-ride scholarship or opt not to go to college at all.

Another common college funding strategy, the Coverdell Education Savings Account, is similar to 529 plans. It is also funded in after-tax dollars, and the benefits are tax free when used for approved educational expenses. The biggest advantage of the ESA is that the funds can be used for pre-college education costs like football uniforms or band instruments. Although this creates a great benefit to fund your children's education, it also probably isn't useful for your education.

But don't fear. You have several opportunities for assistance. Both you and your children should look for scholarship opportunities. You might qualify for money because you are a "nontraditional" student. You might also find funding through your degree choice. Some groups will help support your education if you agree to work in their community when you graduate. Both you and your children may also have a skill or play a sport that can provide some financial assistance.

You and your children might also look for available tax credits. Tax credits are a dollar for dollar lowering of your tax liability and are often more easily obtained if finances are challenging. For more details on education tax credits and additional funding ideas, review IRS Publication 970, "Tax Benefits for Education." Rules are changing rapidly, so work with a financial planner or CPA to be sure you are maximizing your benefits.

Of course, funding your education is only half the challenge. You have to find the time to complete the coursework. Hold a family meeting and explain to everyone why you are going back to school. Tell your goals and dreams to them, along with sharing potential income increases. Then talk about the assistance you will need. It's okay to set aside time and ask not to be disturbed unless someone is bleeding!

Although your children should probably already be helping with the cooking, laundry, and meals, many don't. That's okay, but for as long as it takes you to complete your degree, you will need them to up their game.

Even with the assistance, you likely won't have time to take fifteen hours a semester. That's fine. Take one or two classes at a time, and you will get finished. Additionally, although you want to do well, if you make a grade that is occasionally lower than what you wanted to earn, don't beat yourself up. If you were a straight-A student in high school and you make an occasional B in college, so what? Look at the requirements needed for graduation, and keep your grades higher than those levels. You might consider starting at a community college if the credits will transfer to a four-year institution.

Coursework can be challenging, especially if you've been out of school for many years. If you hit a course that's really difficult, get a tutor. You don't expect other people to be great at everything; you won't be either. Don't beat yourself up. Avoid incompletes, as they are hard to make up, and try hard to pass all your classes.

Finally, here's the cool part. Your dedication to your studies will inspire your children. They may not tell you so, but you will influence how they value education. Who knows —you may even have study dates with them. And together you are both making your futures brighter.

Megan: This chapter gives me so much hope! Maybe I can find time to go back to college.

Jessica: One of my best friends in high school got married rather than going on to college. She's said how much she wishes she could have a professional career. I think I'll encourage her to try to go back.

Kim: My mom went to school after we were born. I remember watching her read textbooks at the kitchen table. She inspired me.

Sharon: Our local university offers free classes when you're over sixty-five. My friends and I enjoy taking them and learning about new topics.

Next Steps

Do you want to go back to school? Start looking at the entrance requirements for your local universities. You can find this on their websites. Be sure the school is accredited, and you might want to avoid for-profit institutions if possible because they can be so expensive. Once you've narrowed down your options, drive there and talk to the counselors. You can do this! Jot your ideas on the following lines.

_____

_____

_____

_____

_____

_____

_____

Widowhood and Divorce

Elizabeth Luxford: The First Colonial Divorcee

DIVORCE in the Puritan Massachusetts Bay Colony did not have the religious stigma you might expect. Remember that Massachusetts was founded because its settlers rejected both Catholicism and Anglicanism. These churches viewed marriage as a religious sacrament, and as a direct result, Puritans decided marriage was a purely civil arrangement.

Still, divorce was uncommon in the Massachusetts Bay Colony, and the guilty party was often punished severely. Such was the fate of James Luxford, husband of Elizabeth Luxford.

Elizabeth and James Luxford were married and expecting their second child when Elizabeth made a shocking discovery. James was already married! He likely had left his first wife in England when he came to Massachusetts. Elizabeth went immediately to the Court of Assistants, the governor's council that decided divorce cases.

Elizabeth was granted the first Puritan divorce in December 1639. James' punishment was harsh. He had to give all of his possessions to Elizabeth, stay out of her sight, sit in the stocks for an hour, and pay fines of one hundred pounds. Perhaps worst of all, he was banned from the Massachusetts Bay Colony.

After her divorce, Elizabeth changed her last name back to Albone, and ultimately remarried. We think of the Puritans as strict, but in cases of divorce, women were not assumed to be guilty. Elizabeth was protected by the legal system and later supported by the church.

James was not out of trouble, however. He served as bailiff to John Winthrop. He overcharged for products, overpaid his friends, and borrowed money from Winthrop's friends, leading them to believe he was acting on behalf of Winthrop, himself. When his crimes were discovered, he was bound to the whipping post, and his ears were cut off. He was banished to England and died in poverty.

Chapter 29

Financial Decisions Under Stress

She still couldn't believe he was gone. She didn't know how or where to begin putting her life back together. Then, the phone calls began. Financial advisers, insurance agents, banks. Everyone wanted her to allow them to help her, of course for a nominal fee. She didn't understand how they knew about it. She was so upset that she hung up on all of them. She turned instead to her own financial team and her closest friends.

HAVE you ever tried to make a decision when you were upset? Unfortunately, I have, and I promise you—it didn't end well. In fact, it never ends well. What was so disarming was I thought I was fine. I knew I was stressed, but I thought I was in control. Later, I realized I wasn't. Whether you are navigating a death or a divorce, you need to be careful with your financial decisions. Your choices today have long-lasting consequences.

Death

Losing a partner through death may be the most stressful event you will ever experience. Every day, you tread fresh hell and wonder if you are losing your mind. I'm very sorry if you are experiencing grief. Unfortunately, in the middle of your pain, you have to make some financial decisions. Even worse, some unscrupulous characters, including a few financial professionals, know you need to make them. Through pressure tactics, misleading guidance, or outright lies, they try to manipulate you out of your money.

One of the worst stories I've heard was of a financial adviser who read the obituaries, sent flowers with his name, and then contacted the family a few weeks after the funeral, asking how he could help. Of course, since he had sent flowers, the family assumed he knew their loved one. He had automatically gained their trust. In fact, he didn't know the person who had died.

There are many steps you can take to avoid being the victim of an adviser like this. If your partner has recently died, your best first move is to postpone as much as possible. Don't make investment decisions, change portfolio allocations, or decide how to use life insurance proceeds yet. There's plenty of time.

Remember to take a trusted friend with you to every meeting you must attend. Have him or her take notes. Don't make any decisions in the meeting. Instead, get away from the office environment that can be intimidating, and review the notes with your friend. Then, make a list of any questions or concerns you have, and require answers to them before you take any actions.

For all couples, both partners need to understand each other's financial life. Look into the details in advance of anything going wrong. For example, even if you handle your money independently, know the name of the other's financial adviser, insurance agent, CPA, and attorney. Have your partner schedule a meeting, so you can meet everyone even if you don't use them professionally. Then, if you need to talk with them alone, you already know them.

Hopefully, you both have also made your list of assets that we discussed earlier in the book. It's important to know how many investment accounts and life insurance policies you must address. You also need to know where the assets and estate documents are located. Finally, don't forget computer passwords! Just recently, a client of mine couldn't access a tax return from the previous year. It was located on her recently deceased spouse's computer that he forgot to include in his list of passwords. As a result, she is hiring an IT professional to try to "hack" the system. It's an unnecessary stress two months after his death.

Also, even if assets appear to be sufficient, check how long it will take for them to change ownership. Sometimes, pension payments don't begin for months, and you may need a plan for paying the bills in the interim.

Once immediate details have been addressed, take some time to heal. Then, in six months to a year (or maybe longer), you'll be in a better mindset to tackle reorganization of your financial affairs. Begin by calculating your spending. This will let you know how to best use the inherited assets rather than just spending them without a plan. In fact, this is a good time to hire a CERTIFIED FINANCIAL PLANNER™ practitioner if you don't already have one. You need to structure your assets to help you meet your new financial goals. It's totally okay if you don't know all of them yet. Take it one day at a time.

Divorce

Loss from divorce is a different stress and adds additional parties who may not be acting in your best interest. You also have the strain of your ex, attorneys, and the financial professionals. Unfortunately, if you are in the middle of a divorce, you don't have the luxury of time. You may be experiencing the emotions around grief, but you can't just focus on healing. You must take actions and make decisions at least until the divorce is final. One of the biggest mistakes people make when their marriage is collapsing is to stall, not wanting to think about the situation. If you aren't careful, the events will proceed without you, leaving you potentially in bad financial straits.

The first thing to remember in a divorce is that you are creating a document to ensure your financial security. Remember, requesting adequate compensation will not keep your ex from returning. You can still reconcile after you have requested a fair income. Often, I hear clients express concern that if they ask for money, the divorce is certain. That's not true. As long as your request is reasonable, I don't believe it will alter future events.

One of the best ways of ensuring both your financial safety and your fairness is to analyze your financial situation. Before you and your attorney file anything related to asset division (not just legal separation), work with a CERTIFIED FINANCIAL PLANNER™ practitioner. You should determine both your current cash flow needs, your spouse's cash flow needs, children's college funding requirements, and your retirement needs.

Although your analysis of your spouse's need is not directly helpful, it could be a useful tool if you are the one paying the alimony. If your spouse proposes a noticeably higher payment than what you have calculated, you could look at it more closely before you agree to it. Current cash flow and college funding impacts alimony, while retirement calculations will be needed to determine your needs after your working years. Although there is no guarantee the judge will use your calculations, you certainly won't get the amounts you need if you haven't computed them.

Calculating cash flow during a divorce can be stressful. Again, employ a trusted friend. Go over your current spending with this person to be sure you haven't omitted anything. Additionally, consider any lifestyle changes that will be necessary and adjust your anticipated spending appropriately.

Stress impacts our ability to think clearly and make good decisions. When you are dealing with the stress of death or divorce, your actions need to be taken carefully. In both cases, surround yourself with people you can trust and the appropriate professionals to help ensure your best financial future.

This section of the book will help you through your transition. We will explore many topics in the following chapters. I know you might not care right now, but you will at some point.

> Megan: My divorce left me aching. I didn't expect it to hurt as bad as it did. We weren't getting along, but it's the hardest thing I've ever done.

Jessica: I've made so many bad decisions when I was under a lot of stress. Thank God, I've never been widowed or divorced, but less stress than that impacted my judgment. Once, it caused me to wreck my car.

Kim: The most deceptive part of stress is when you don't know how messed up you are. Fortunately, we have a tight circle of friends. We get each other through whatever life dishes out.

Sharon: I was horrified by how many so-called financial advisers called me shortly after my husband died. Everyone wanted to schedule a meeting to "help." Fortunately, I knew not to take them up on their offers.

Next Steps

If you are under stress right now, surround yourself with support. Family, friends, and appropriate professionals can help make a bad situation better. If you're the friend, listen and learn. You can help her with research and encourage her to take time. Jot some notes here to help create a plan.

Chapter 30

Steps If Divorce Is Impending

She didn't want to believe it was true. Her marriage was supposed to last forever. But she knew she couldn't take it anymore. Growing apart led to constant bickering, then yelling, and now silence. She wasn't sure who would file first or how long it would take. But she knew one of them would file for divorce soon.

SOMETIMES, a spouse will file for divorce unexpectedly. More often, though, both partners know they're growing apart. Maybe you're the one wanting the divorce and are considering filing. If so, you want to complete several steps before you take official action.

First, gather copies of your financial records. You will need bank, brokerage, and pension statements, deeds, trusts, insurance policies, annuities—literally any and all financial documents. Rather than taking them with you to meetings, or even removing them from your home where the absence might be noticed, you may want to take copies of the originals. You can always take pictures of documents with your phone. You'll need these records to be certain you receive your fair share in the financial settlement. Organizing the paperwork in advance will help ensure you don't miss anything.

Additionally, you will need money—both for living expenses after the break-up and attorney fees. You don't want your spouse to prevent you from accessing your joint accounts. If you are afraid divorce is approaching and if it's safe for you to do it, open an account in your name and then gradually move some money into it. If you can't open an account, you can withdraw cash. Withdrawing small amounts at a time might draw less attention. Just be careful. You will need to determine a strategy that fits your circumstances.

If you are caught off guard by your spouse, though, make a stop by the bank the first day you are separated to withdraw some cash for living expenses. It's not wrong to take care of yourself.

Review the assets you own jointly and separately. This will require you to have knowledge of your state's laws on property ownership. Some states are common law, while others are community property. The thorns and details on the subject exceed this book, but you should research your state and talk to an attorney. You will need to know which assets are yours exclusively and which are split with your spouse.

If you fear an impending divorce, get a post office box. Then, make a list of all the important mail that comes to you and copy the senders' addresses. If you don't want to change your address yet, you don't have to, but at least you have everything organized. You don't want personal mail or bills coming to the home if your spouse still has access to the mailbox. If you're still living in the home, sending the mail somewhere else will eliminate a potential crisis.

You may need access to additional funds while you are in the middle of your divorce. Once you have a post office box, apply for a credit card in your name only and send the statements to the box. Although I never advise living off credit cards, you may need access to more cash than you have. Plan to pay the card balance off in full as soon as you receive your divorce settlement.

Additionally, check your credit report and score. While moving your mail will ensure you see your bills, checking your credit report will let you know if your name is on any debt, old or new. Originally, a debt might have been agreeable to both of you. However, now that you are dividing your property, you want to be careful that you don't receive assets in the settlement that come with loans and large payments unless you want them. For example, you might want to keep the house, but if it's highly mortgaged, the actual value might be low. Possessions are often divided somewhat haphazardly in a divorce, and emotions tend to rule the day. Be certain to subtract any loans to be sure that you and your spouse are receiving equivalently valued assets.

You will also want to confirm that your name isn't on any loans that might have been made without your knowledge. Be certain you check your credit report again, right before and after the divorce is settled. You don't want any new transactions to slip by. Conversely, be sure your name hasn't been removed from a credit card without your knowledge.

Additionally, if you are still married and covered by your spouse's health insurance, now would be a good time for any doctor appointments, glasses updates, and prescription refills. Of course, you will need your own insurance in effect once you are legally single, but if you currently have good coverage, take advantage of it. Getting your own coverage should be relatively straight forward. Your divorce will count as a change of life circumstance, so you should be able to enroll in your employer's insurance or secure Affordable Care Act (Obamacare) coverage, assuming you meet the minimum income requirements that take you outside the Medicaid system.

Finally, put together a good team. You will need a divorce attorney, but that likely won't be enough. Calculating your living expenses is more the work of a financial planner. As you are interviewing attorneys, see if they are open to working with a CFP® pro. You may want a CPA, also, depending on the complexity of your taxes. You will want to go to court with your case as strong as possible before the assets are divided. If you overlook issues and have to go back to court later, there's no guarantee your spouse will have the same available resources to adjust your settlement.

Getting a divorce is stressful. By taking some steps prior to filing, you will be less likely to forget something important.

Megan: I didn't have enough money to put together a good team. I avoided my attorney because he was so expensive. I might have gotten a better settlement if I had spent more time determining what we would need.

Jessica: I can't imagine trying to make a list of everything I owned, especially if I were older and had more assets. I would think you should start that process as early as you can.

Kim: I'm glad Peggy warned women about staying safe. We have a friend who literally left with the shirt on her back and the money in her purse. She didn't have a choice because her husband became violent. At least she's alive.

> Sharon: I remember the day when a woman couldn't get a credit card on her own. Times aren't perfect, but they are better.

Next Steps

If you're afraid divorce is imminent, decide which of these steps you can take safely. Jot your ideas either here or somewhere you can review if the need occurs.

_____

_____

_____

_____

_____

_____

Chapter 31

Life Insurance and Lump Sums

Most people smile when they see a large balance in their bank account. But she didn't. All she could imagine was that last fast kiss as her husband left to go to work. "See you tonight," he'd said. But she didn't see him that night. The following days were a blur, and she signed papers she was told she had to sign. Too soon after his death, a large check arrived from the insurance company. She didn't want to cash it, but her best friend told her she needed to do it. Now, every time she looked at her account online, she felt sick to her stomach. She hated that money.

Many times, we daydream about what we would do if we suddenly acquired a large lump sum of money. We might take a trip or go on a shopping spree. We might help our favorite charity or pay for college education for the children.

However, sometimes, we receive money we don't want. When we inherit a life insurance policy or we receive a lump sum settlement in a divorce, we might rather not have the money at all.

Too often, the stress of acquiring money in these situations causes us to make terrible decisions. Remember that both life insurance proceeds and divorce settlements should be calculated in a way to provide financial security for many years.

And yet sometimes we are so upset about receiving the money that we spend it as quickly as possible. Why? Because we don't want what it represents, and seeing it reminds us of our sadness. So we spend it. All of it. And just like that, there aren't enough resources to last the rest of our lives.

Just as damaging to our financial future can be the advice and recommendations of others. Some of the people who think they know what we should do with our newfound wealth may mean well. However, their lack of financial knowledge or understanding of our needs makes them ill equipped to give us the best advice. Additionally, family and friends may feel entitled to some of the money, and telling them "No" can be difficult.

Most dangerous are those people who don't mean us well. They want to exploit our grief and earn a tidy profit from it. These people are often financial professionals, but they may take the form of many other types of specialists.

So what should you do? You're already heartbroken, and you don't want to make a bad decision, so how can you avoid these pitfalls?

The answer is easy—don't do more than what you absolutely have to do, and don't sign any contracts until the world makes more sense.

You will have some bills and issues that will require your immediate financial attention. Choose the person you trust the most to help you navigate those situations. Then, don't make any other major financial decisions for at least six months. Maybe longer.

For example, don't rush out and purchase a piece of property or pay off an existing mortgage. Don't try to make investment choices—your risk tolerance will be completely off balance, and you will find you're either extraordinarily conservative or overly aggressive.

Instead, let everything rock along, and don't do anything you will regret. Ignore anyone who pressures you. You need to work through the grieving process, at least somewhat, before you try to address any financial "to-dos" in your life. Time won't heal your wounds, but it will help you gain some clarity of thought. Then, you will be in a better position to make decisions about how to handle the money.

Megan: I didn't receive a large settlement in my divorce. In fairness, he didn't have a lot of money either.

Jessica: My friend Jill's father wanted a divorce, and he left her mom much poorer than they had been before. It changed both of them. Jill became more distant, and I never knew why. I need to call her and try to reestablish our friendship.

Kim: I suspect people also feel guilty about suddenly having money after a loss. Those are circumstances that could lead to unhealthy behavior.

Sharon: It's sad watching someone waste money they inherit, but it's worse seeing them struggle because their spouse didn't think insurance was necessary.

Next Steps

If you find yourself acquiring a large lump sum of cash as the result of a tragic or stressful situation, move slowly. Jot down the items that must be resolved immediately, and leave everything else alone until you feel more in control of your life.

Chapter 32

Negotiating Settlements

She didn't ask for this divorce. The marriage had been anything but peaceful, but she still wanted to try to salvage things. Her friends reminded her that he had filed and had apparently already moved on with his personal life. Still, she didn't want to make him mad by asking for a large settlement. When the financial planner told her how much she needed to be financially secure, she didn't want to ask for that much. Maybe if she stayed "reasonable," he'd come back.

IF YOU ARE FACING DIVORCE, I am so sorry. I know you may feel as if your world is unravelling, and you are trying to make decisions while every fiber of your being hates what is happening.

As you work your way through this personal crisis, I want you to be careful that you don't let your stress and sadness impact the financial decisions you need to make. Please share this chapter with a close friend who can help you understand what steps to take to ensure your financial security.

Remember that your divorce is simply the legal side of your separation. The terms of the divorce do not have anything to do with the grief you are feeling. And yet, often your emotions wreak havoc on your decision-making process.

For example, I hear women say that they don't care about the terms of the divorce. They just want it over with. They say things similar to, "Let him have everything. I don't want it. I just want this nightmare to end."

Please, please, please get your best friend involved here because she or he sees the situation more clearly than you do. You may not care at all about the money now, but you will later. The settlement you and your spouse sign will have a major impact on your financial well-being. Research shows that women suffer financially much more after divorce than men do. There are likely a number of reasons, but I believe that one of the primary problems is that women don't obtain reasonable settlements. A friend may better help you think through issues.

Even if you want to obtain a property division that supports you sufficiently, you may feel guilty asking for the money. You may be afraid that people will perceive you as greedy, especially if the divorce was at least partially your idea. You have to put that fear aside. Assuming adequate resources, the amount of settlement you should receive should be based on your cash flow needs—your ability to maintain a lifestyle at least somewhat similar to the one you had prior to the divorce.

As a result, like so many other parts of financial planning, your divorce settlement starts with your cash flow. If you have completed your spending analysis from the first section, then you know how much you spend each month. That figure will strongly impact how much settlement you will need.

You may expect your attorney to ask for an amount that will fit your needs, but you need to remember two things. First, lawyers can't request an amount if you haven't computed it, and then you must provide that information to them. Give your attorney a cash flow analysis so he or she will know what you spend each month.

Second, attorneys aren't financial planners. Some attorneys use financial experts in their practice, but most don't. As a result, you may want to use your financial planner or find a new one. Remember, Chapter Twelve provides you with tools to use when you want to hire a planner. Sometimes, especially if your old adviser had a closer relationship with your spouse than with you, you might want a change. It's also quite possible that your former planner won't want to be accused of being partial. She may not feel she can ethically maintain the relationship with you and your spouse.

Truthfully, I think it's possible for both parties to maintain a relationship with their existing financial planner. Planning shouldn't be biased in favor of either partner, and the planner could show attorneys the cash flow needs of both parties. Unfortunately, this idea usually sounds better in theory than it works in practice because of the temperature of the emotions.

However, engaging your planner is important. They can help with the financial settlement of a divorce in a number of ways.

• The planner likely already knows the expenses and cash flow. This data can be used to compute both alimony and child support, especially if the planner can create an education funding table showing how much money will be needed to fund college for the children.

• The planner can also help determine whether or not one spouse needs to provide a life insurance policy to cover expenses that might not be available in a liquid format in the case of his or her demise. Such a policy can be especially useful when one of the spouses owns a business.

• The planner can help even out the assets by showing the future value of investment accounts using a realistic rate of return. These are then compared to the current value of possessions that might have a different growth rate. For example, a house worth $300,000 and an investment portfolio worth $300,000 have the same value today. However, the investment portfolio has a much higher growth potential. The assets aren't worth the same amount, in "real" dollars. The house is worth quite a bit less. Additionally, the home is not liquid and cannot easily pay for retirement expenses. The spouse who lives there might need to move in order to sell the house to generate funds. The error isn't always made deliberately by either side, but the outcome can be detrimental to one party or the other, especially ten or twenty years down the road.

Divorce can be overwhelming and depressing, but you still have to look out for your own best interests. Having a fear of making your ex angry shouldn't impact what you request, and calculating an adequate settlement won't stop a potential reconciliation. It will just keep you financially safe.

～

Megan: When I was calculating my living expenses, I didn't spend enough time on the list. I didn't mean to overlook items, but it was just so hard to focus.

Jessica: I knew it was important for me to understand my money, but I'm not sure I realized how significant financial planning can be.

Kim: Wow, I know a lot of divorced women. I don't remember any of them mentioning running a full-blown cash flow analysis.

Sharon: So many women think they might reconcile with their ex. I've never seen it work, but I know it's led to some bad settlement agreements.

Next Steps

Calculating your need after a divorce involves formulas similar to calculating your retirement need and your net worth. On the following lines, jot some notes about what assets are yours, what are held jointly, and what liability (debt) is attached to any of them.

Chapter 33

Stress Spending

After they fought, she alternated between being angry and sad. Being alone made her antsy, so during her lunch hours she went to the mall. A new pair of shoes made her feel better, as did fresh lipstick and a crisp, white blouse. As the fights increased, so did her credit card balance.

Do you ever spend money when you're angry? Have you had a fight with your partner or a bad day at work and headed to the mall? Maybe on the way home from helping your mom you've stopped for a new pair of shoes. Or you've been worried about your kids and bought a new laptop.

Popular culture uses the term "retail therapy," and there's much truth to the expression. Stress can cause people to develop poor financial behavior.

The roots of why this happens can be found in two closely related disciplines: behavioral finance and interior finance. Without going into too much detail, the underlying premise of both fields is that we do not respond rationally to money. The concept of "the rational investor" is one of the major tenets of modern portfolio theory (MPT). MPT says that everything else being equal, investors will always choose the investment that offers the most return for the least risk.

It's a beautiful, elegant theorem. There's just one problem: frequently, it's not true. Often, people will choose the investment that their parents already own, or they will invest in something that they heard about at work or from friends. Sometimes, investors buy newsletters and simply purchase the recommended list. Stock market bubbles are excellent proof that people are not always logical in their investment decisions.

This same non-rational behavior can be seen in other parts of people's financial lives. Sometimes, faced with significant credit card debt, people don't slow their spending. They actually speed it up. Children follow the financial patterns of their parents.

Worse, sometimes we create money scripts for ourselves. We announce that we are just "not good at money." Have you ever heard someone say this, or have you said it yourself? This talk sabotages our actions because it gives us an excuse for bad behavior. Please stop saying that you are just not good at money.

Instead, I want you to start saying that you are great with money. Now, if you think this sounds arrogant, just say it to yourself every morning in the mirror as you get ready for the day. I know it sounds like the hokiest kind of self-help or a Saturday Night Live skit. But do it anyway. You will tend to rise and fall to the level of your words.

Many people spend money in reaction to the issues in their lives. There doesn't need to be a correlation between the stress we are experiencing and what we purchase. Under stress none of us make logical choices, and we buy things to make ourselves feel better.

If you can afford what you purchase, there is probably

little issue with your behavior. However, I think you would be wise to at least recognize what is occurring. The real crisis happens if you can't afford what you're buying. Unfortunately, the ability to afford your purchases doesn't seem to impact most peoples' financial behavior. When people are stressed, they spend money.

Closely related to stress spending is revenge spending. This kind of behavior is dangerous, because it is spending designed to create a precarious financial situation.

The first manifestation of revenge spending is when your partner purchases something that you don't think he or she needs. Then you go out and purchase something that you are sure they won't think you need, either. If they can have what they want, then, by God, you can too.

Obviously, this is destructive. If you believe your partner is wasting money you both can't afford, talk to him or her when emotions aren't high. Remember how we talked about creating a budget as a family? This is a great time to talk to your partner about your available resources and what either of you can afford to spend.

Related to this, it's always smart to determine how much spending money is available to each of you. Many couples have found that the easiest way to avoid financial conflicts is to determine, in advance, how much spending money is possible apiece. Then, the other partner shouldn't criticize how that money is spent. If you think your partner's spending is unnecessary, as long as it's his or her discretionary money, you are probably best served to keep your opinions to yourself.

The second kind of revenge spending occurs when you are angry with your partner. You go shopping, not caring what you spend, because you want to get even with what they have done to you.

This is a common, destructive financial behavior. You

would be better off trying to resolve the situation that caused your anger. This may involve professional assistance, and there are financial planners who work in conjunction with marriage counselors. I'm not trying to offer solutions here. Just be aware that if you are engaging in revenge spending, you should try to resolve the underlying issues. Spending the money won't make you happy; it will just increase your debt.

The third kind of revenge spending happens so often that many people don't recognize it. Rather than the "wronged party" doing the spending, make-up spending involves the person who angered their partner. That partner buys gifts to try to right a wrong. Giving flowers because you have hurt someone's feelings is so common it's a stereotype.

Think about what you are doing for a minute or what you are asking your partner to do. You're trying to solve hurt feelings with money. Now, I'm not unkind. I'm not opposed to sending flowers, but I wish you would do this after a long talk about what went wrong and how to keep it from happening again. That is, send flowers as a last, final step. I don't want flowers to be sent repeatedly when the situation doesn't change. That kind of pattern is destructive, and eventually we all know the flowers won't be enough. The conflict will escalate, and the price of the gifts may too. Even if you need to use a relationship counselor, work out your disagreements with your partner. Then, together, you can send the flowers to the therapist!

Stress spending is not only bad for your relationship, but also destructive to your financial bottom line. Look at your patterns to see whether or not your life situations control your purchases. Gaining control of your actions will help you feel empowered.

Megan: Wow, I can't believe how much this chapter describes me when I was married. Every time we had a fight, I went shopping. I didn't mean it as revenge. Buying things just made me feel better.

Jessica: I can relate to stress spending! For me, it's any stress I'm experiencing, not just relationship based. I probably need to find a healthier outlet.

Kim: Sam and I have a good relationship, but, early on, we had a fight. I was so angry that I went shopping and purchased a digital camera and printer. I have another friend who buys shoes. It can get out of hand.

Sharon: My husband and I had a great relationship. We fought occasionally, but I never wanted to go shopping. I think my grandmother's experience during the Depression shaped both my mom's and my attitude toward money.

Next Steps

Do you tend to shop when you are upset? I'm not going to tell you to stop, but you might want to be more aware of your actions. Jot down how many items you purchased under stress during the last year. How much did you spend, and could you afford it?

_____

_____

Chapter 34

Talking to a Partner About Money

They had a great marriage. They had fun, still went on dates, and loved their kids. In most ways, it was a healthy relationship. Except they couldn't talk easily about money. He got mad when she went shopping, and she was angry when he played poker with the guys. They could afford their hobbies, at least most of the time. However, that didn't stop the snide comments.

Did you know that money issues are the leading cause of divorce? Some say money problems are more toxic to a marriage than infidelity. How can you avoid your marriage becoming a statistic? Begin talking about money early on in your relationship.

I would not recommend talking about your income or asking about student loans on your first date. Additionally, I wouldn't expect your date to talk about money, either. If either of you does, there's a good chance there will never be a second date! But you should begin to talk about money if it looks like your relationship is becoming serious.

Discomfort with talking about money is somewhat generational. I believe younger women are less bothered than those of us a bit older. Many of us still haven't completely broken the old stereotype of "nice girls don't talk about money."

Even worse, when women have clear financial plans or a comfortable salary, some may almost be afraid to talk about it. It seems counterintuitive. How can success cause shame? It shouldn't, and I keep reading that women's expectations are changing, and they are less concerned with appealing to traditional stereotypes. However, I find the stress of success exists in some of the young women I know. These women are ambitious, mind you, but their success and drive still make them uncomfortable. I guess old habits die hard. Hopefully, the responses and concerns are going away.

However, fear of success isn't the only restraining factor. Some women worry about how their accomplishments will impact potential relationships, and my advice is not to worry about it.

Yes, some people may be intimidated by a woman with a good job. But if you're a successful woman and intimidate your love interest, maybe you should keep the job and end the relationship!

Whether or not it feels awkward, before you agree to a relationship where you share expenses with someone, you should have a clear idea of each other's financial situation. At the least, you should both know

- The other person's salary
- Any student loan debt
- Any credit card debt
- Any other significant, outstanding debt
- Basic spending habits and hobbies.

Neither of you should consider money a topic not to discuss. If it becomes an organic part of your lives together, you will be much less likely to run into financial discord later.

Even before you're living under the same roof, you will need to make some decisions on how you plan to pay the bills. Maybe one of you wants to take the responsibility to handle all of them, or perhaps you will decide to split them. Just be sure you are clear on the process. When my husband and I got married, he told me he would pay the bills. Well, I had lived alone for ten years. I didn't need that! So I told him no, I would pay them. But we hadn't made a real plan, and I didn't give it a lot of thought. Apparently, neither did he. About forty-five days after we were married, we began to get late notices. Neither of us had paid the bills! So be sure you're clear on everyone's role.

Paying expenses is just the beginning. Do you create joint bank accounts (checking and savings) or keep individual ones? Are paychecks deposited into a joint account? How do you want to handle spending money? The more you address the details of your finances, the easier the process becomes.

Issues don't end after you are established in your relationship. Although you may have been happily married for many years with no money discord, both parties need to understand the details of their finances. Something could happen to one of you, and the other party would need to be able to continue without any financial disasters. Many women fear being alone, and financial strain makes it even worse.

Even if your partner is alive, you still need to understand the finances of your home. Despite the advances women have made in financial stewardship, I am horrified by how many of them still think it's funny that they don't know how to pay the monthly bills. They assure me that their husbands take care of everything. However, if those women find themselves alone, they are thrown into a situation that is much more complicated than it needs to be.

You never need to be part of this statistic. If you have a

partner who takes care of the finances, that's great! However, you should periodically take an active role in reviewing the bills and paying them. You need to know where the bank accounts are located and what bills are due. This is easier if you organize the obligations to be paid in a simple way. If you bring in the mail, start sorting the bills from the rest of what's sent and put them in a specific place.

Of course, bills don't just come in the mail anymore. You and your partner need to make a list of your liabilities, the websites, and the login and password information. Periodically, you should pay the bills together.

Anytime there is a change to your monthly cash flow, you and your partner need to review it. If you buy a house, it's easy to remember. But if you add another kind of bill, it's important that you both know who issued the credit, how much is owed, and when it is due.

This can be a little more confusing than it sounds, because when you purchase something on an extended, no-interest plan, many times you are acquiring a credit card. The card company may have no correlation with the store, so you might see an envelope and not recognize it as a purchase. The worst outcome is you throw it away without opening it, assuming it's junk mail!

If you don't like paying the bills, and you have someone else willing to do it for you, that's great. You just need to be able to pay them. I consider financial knowledge similar to automotive maintenance. Just because you know how to change the oil in your car doesn't mean you ever have to do it. But you should have the ability if it is necessary.

∼

Megan: We fought a lot about money, even though there were other issues, as well. I wanted to save for our future, and he liked to celebrate the day. His way was fun, but I knew we would never get ahead.

Jessica: I think I'm single partly because I don't want to deal with someone else's money issues right now. I've had relationships before, and often the guy is intimidated by how focused I am. I want to wait until I meet someone who can accept me for myself!

Kim: Before Sam and I moved in together, we had a long talk about money. We don't agree on everything, but we understand each other.

Sharon: Peggy didn't talk about the generational differences between how couples communicate. I think lack of talking about money is probably more common in people over sixty. Back in the day, it just wasn't done.

Next Steps

One of my goals for this section is to help you avoid divorce. If you and your partner don't talk about money, then this chapter is a good time to start. Jot some notes on ideas for beginning the conversation.

Chapter 35

Financial Habits from Childhood

"Finish your dinner. There are starving children in another part of the world." Although this warning isn't as commonly heard at dinner tables today, you may have heard it growing up. The command to eat your vegetables wasn't strong enough on its own. You needed the guilt of having food when others were hungry! That sense of responsibility didn't end for many people. The need to eat everything still haunts them, and some suffer from obesity because they are unable to turn off that voice. Childhood lessons and commands are powerful. Not only do they impact eating habits, but they also govern how we view money.

WE REMEMBER the lessons we were taught as children. We might not remember why we got up and went into the other room, but we can recite word for word the lessons we learned when we were young. Usually this is good. We learned the alphabet, our multiplication tables, the presidents of the United States in order, and The Golden Rule. If we watched Saturday morning cartoons back in the day, we can even sing the preamble to the Constitution!

We also remember what we were taught, or not taught, about money and the people who were wealthy or poor. Some of us had parents who told us that rich people exploited workers to increase their wealth. Others explained that people were poor because they didn't work hard enough.

Maybe money was a source of constant household tension, with behaviors suggesting there was never enough. Perhaps your mother hid her spending from your father. You saw it, but you knew not to say anything. Your parents might have suggested you go into a career because it had good earning potential. Although your parents could have had healthy financial practices, maybe money was a subject that your family didn't talk about at all.

Why am I including a chapter on your childhood financial memories in this section? It's simple. I would like to try to help you avoid divorce! Remember that statistic about financial stress being the number one cause of couples splitting up? The issues can be deep rooted.

You and your spouse both have childhood memories of money. You may not be aware of how powerfully they still impact your behaviors. Sometimes, we continue our parents' money patterns, and sometimes, we choose to do the opposite.

For example, maybe you grew up in a home where your mother and father fought about how much money the other spent. You might react to this by being overly worried about every dime. Or perhaps you learn to hide your own purchases from your partner.

On the other hand, maybe your spouse grew up in a household that saw interest in money as greedy or, possibly, a sin. Unconsciously, he or she may create a lifestyle that doesn't pay attention to finances. Conversely, possibly they found the behavior upsetting, and they grew up to be materialistic.

When you understand your partner's financial background, behaviors can move from annoying (or worse) to understandable. Remember, though, for either of you to be able to share your beliefs, you first must recognize them in yourselves.

Examining your ideas about money can be uncomfortable. A good place to begin is to think about immediate reactions you have to different financial circumstances. How do you feel about each of the following items:

• Having debt?
• Making major purchases?
• Delaying the purchase of something you want, so you can pay for it in cash?
• Working in a job you find rewarding but doesn't pay well?
• Working in a job you hate but pays great?
• Giving your children money?
• Inheriting money?
• Giving to charity?
• Earning significantly more or less than your partner?
• Discovering your partner lied to you about money?
• Reacting the way you do when your partner tells you the truth about money?

These questions are just the beginning. However, they will start to give you some insight into how you view money. Ask your partner to complete these questions, as well. Then, talk to each other about your answers. Choose a time that isn't in conjunction with a disagreement, and make the commitment not to get upset or correct each other. You both feel the way you feel, and the goal of the exercise is to open financial communication, not yell.

Once you begin to explore your money beliefs, they

become easier to recognize. If they seem unhealthy to you, you can begin to take steps to act mindfully, not automatically, in your financial decisions and behaviors. Changing beliefs from childhood can be difficult. If you are interested in learning more tools, you can read books in the fields of behavioral finance and interior finance. If the situation is too painful, you might consider a financial therapist. Since this is an emerging profession, there may be no local practitioners, and you might need to work with someone remotely. Of course, do extensive research, and interview anyone you are considering.

When you and your partner understand each other's financial beliefs and choose to work as a team rather than as adversaries, your relationship will strengthen. Taking money fights off the table will go a long way to ensure a long future together.

Megan: My mom was divorced too. I was always just a little afraid we wouldn't have enough money, even though she never said that. I want to get my situation more stable and then talk to my daughter about money, so she doesn't feel like I did.

Jessica: I'm sure I was influenced by my mother. She was divorced from my dad and had to learn to be independent before she met my stepdad. I've always wanted to be as strong as she is.

Kim: I only recently came to realize how many of my financial beliefs come from my childhood. My parents valued helping people more than being financially secure, themselves. Although I would do almost anything to help a friend, I draw boundaries. I saw what happened when those lines didn't exist.

Sharon: My grandmother grew up in the Depression. She never wasted anything and tended to buy items in surplus. I do the same. Although I'm alone, I always own at least ten rolls of paper towels. It's silly, but I'm always a little afraid of running out of items.

Next Steps

If you want to explore your money beliefs, complete the questionnaire in the chapter, even if you're single. If you're in a relationship, you can learn about each other and look for areas of compatibility and potential strife through your answers. With your new knowledge, annoying habits might make more sense. Jot some notes about your plans.

Chapter 36

Titling and Estate Planning

After their dad died, their mom fell apart. Their kids helped her with the financial documents—transferring assets into her name. But somehow, they forgot the house. Or maybe they felt funny asking to place their name on her deed, so they never addressed it. Days turned into months turned into years. Finally, mom joined dad. The home was still in mom's name and was subject to probate, a long and expensive process. Why hadn't they talked to her about changing the title before she died?

I'M ALWAYS amazed how much financial literature assumes you are married. With the prevalence of divorce, the potential for widowhood, or simply the decision not to marry, most women will be single for at least part of their adult life. Being unmarried has financial planning consequences. For starters, you have to make everything "work" on one income. However, it's more complex than that. One area that deserves particular attention when you're single is estate planning.

We talked about basic estate documents in Chapter Twenty-Five, when we reviewed how to help your parents put together an estate plan. However, it's likely that one of your folks—probably mom—will survive her spouse. Additionally, maybe you are single or divorced. How do you structure your estate to avoid as many complications as possible?

First, remember that our culture has a bias toward spouses. They are assumed to know about end of life wishes, and they are probably already on the financial documents, making the powers of attorney for finance less necessary. The same indulgence, however, is not given to domestic partnerships, parent/child relationships, or friendships.

Domestic partnerships, more commonly called "living together," have few legal protections. The lack of structure can be tricky by itself, and if parents or other family members try to intervene, the results can be disastrous.

I've heard stories where one member of a long-term domestic partnership dies. If the family didn't approve of the relationship or simply wanted to lay claim to the assets, they took the surviving partner to court. As a result, in addition to losing the relationship, the survivor also lost his or her home and other financial assets. All because of titling mistakes.

Often, people don't talk to an attorney when they sign a title. Instead, they follow most of the common conventions that go along with their marital status. That might not be the best decision. I want you to talk to an attorney about how your assets are titled and the estate implications of your choices. If you are living with someone, it's even more important because titling is complicated.

Different kinds of titles have distinctive characteristics. Some titling assumes that the asset is held entirely by both parties, and the title automatically goes to the survivor if someone dies. Some titling, however, assumes that you own the percentage share of an asset that corresponds to how much money you contributed to the purchase. As a result, if one partner is wealthy and purchases the home, the other partner could find herself without somewhere to live if the title doesn't allow her to keep the house in a "survivorship" situation.

Additionally, living wills and powers of attorney for healthcare and finance take on an added significance when couples are unmarried. The Terri Schiavo case was contentious because the boyfriend and the mother disagreed on Terri's treatment. He believed she would not want to live in her impaired condition, while her mother wanted to save her life at all costs. Had Terri simply had a living will, the national drama and pain for all parties could have been avoided.

Although not always true, I've noticed that unmarried couples tend to hold assets in just their name while married couples are more likely to title items jointly. There are potentially sound reasons for taking this position, but it can lead to estate issues, raising the likelihood of probate.

To avoid this from occurring, three types of asset distribution usually avoid probate—beneficiary, titling, and trust. If you are the sole beneficiary of an account, the asset will not be probated. If the titling allows the asset to pass directly to you, you also can avoid the process. Finally, when assets are held in trust, they pass outside probate.

However, none of those simple distribution situations may exist for your asset. And having assets just in a will often requires probate before they are released. Without additional care in titling, automobiles and homes can fall into this situation, as they did for the children of the woman in our story.

When couples are married, assets are often held in joint tenancy with a survivorship mechanism. The problem occurs after the death of the first spouse. Now, the surviving spouse needs to go into all the assets and change the titles to put someone else in as survivor, beneficiary, or trust recipient. Often, children fill these roles, and the process is relatively straightforward.

However, if someone is single and never had children, deciding who will receive your assets is more complicated. Maybe you want to leave them to a friend. Maybe you want to leave them to charity.

Powers of attorney are also trickier for women without children. Although you should always ask someone if they are willing to hold a power of attorney for you, it is even more critical when it's your friend, not your child. Please don't surprise someone by putting them into a role of helping if you are incapacitated.. And don't feel angry if they tell you no. It's a lot of responsibility, and not everyone wants it.

So to sum it up, the law has mechanisms that will allow you to protect yourself, make end of life decisions, and give your possessions to whomever you choose. However, your personal situation, and what steps you take to direct the disposition of what you own, will dictate whether the process will be fairly straightforward or more complex. No one likes to think about these scenarios, but take some time to organize your estate plan. Work with an attorney and be sure that you have resolved any situations, especially if your circumstances are tricky.

～

Megan: I need to take steps to protect Charlotte in case something happens to me.

Jessica: Right now, I have my mom as my beneficiary to my retirement plan. I should probably add her to my car as well. That's the only big asset I own.

Kim: Sam and I created a detailed estate plan a few years ago. Our parents consider us both family, but we still need legal protection and clear directives.

Sharon: My daughter is my financial power of attorney, but my children share power of attorney for healthcare. That way, neither of them has to feel solely and personally responsible for making decisions on my behalf. I think it's kinder to both of them.

Next Steps

If you don't have your end-of-life documents in place, you need to remedy that, whether you're single or married. If you are newly single, review all your existing documents. You don't want your ex holding a medical power of attorney! Jot some notes on the steps you need to take.

_____

_____

_____

Chapter 37

When It's Just You Again

She hated doing everything alone. She no longer had a "plus one," and she found she avoided events. She despised calling maintenance people and scheduling repairs. But most of all, she felt alone in her decision-making process. Maybe her spouse hadn't always given perfect advice, but it had been easier making decisions together. Now, it was just her.

SUDDENLY, you're single again. Even if you are a capable, persistent woman, the idea can be daunting. You have a lot of adjusting to do, and there are some areas you might want to be aware of.

First, before you create long-term monthly spending habits, I hope you complete a cash flow analysis. You may find that you spend quite a bit more or less than you did when you were married. A quick check here can give you an opportunity to make a course correction before it gets too late.

Next, be careful with any investment decisions you make. I find that most people are either overly aggressive or overly conservative after a major life change. Try to keep your investment portfolio "middle of the road," and complete a risk tolerance form two to three times a year until you find yourself scoring similar results repeatedly.

Additionally, try to avoid making any major, irrevocable financial decisions for a period of time. For example, once you choose to annuitize an account (or in English, convert it from a lump sum to a consistent stream of income in an annuity), you can't undo that decision, and you sharply curtail your options. Just leave things alone for a while if that's at all possible. You're still trying to figure out the new you.

Check all your listed beneficiaries. Be sure to include your insurance policies, retirement account at work, and any personal retirement accounts. You might still have your spouse's name on a bank account or a bank box or something else that I haven't thought to list here. In cases of divorce, it's especially important to get his name off everything unless you have a legal reason that you can't do it.

Finally, it's possible that despite your best efforts, money is tighter than it used to be. You may not be able to purchase items for your children like before. You may have to explain that their lives will be a little different. This can be a difficult conversation, but trust me—they are smarter than you might think they are. They know what's going on. Rather than treating it like a crisis, make it an adventure. Have contests to see who can save the most money out of what they thought they would spend that week. Make cooking a fun, family project. These changes can be stressful, or they can be turned into opportunities to spend time together and help each other.

Divorce often creates particularly difficult situations regarding the kids. Too many times after a divorce, the spouse who sees the children less thinks they can keep their love by buying expensive gifts. In less healthy environments, some ex-spouses will purposely give better gifts than the spouse who has custody. If you are dealing with either of these situations, don't let it get to you. Specifically, don't take it out on your children. Don't be critical of your ex in front of them. And unless there's a solid reason, don't take away the expensive gift. Just continue to stress the importance of living a fulfilled, caring life. Your children may love the gifts, but they aren't as easily fooled as you might think. For the most part, you will just have to ignore your ex's behavior.

I want to end this section with one last concern. Most people enter a new relationship after being widowed or divorced, at least eventually. But be careful that you don't make decisions based on your financial discomfort. I have seen women, unfortunately of all ages, so uncertain about making financial decisions that they entered relationships shortly after they found themselves alone. They wanted someone else to take care of everything, or they were terribly lonely.

I know you're overwhelmed. I know this is awful. But you need to learn how to take care of your own money. Don't begin to date someone out of fear of being alone. This behavior will tend to lead to your making bad decisions. Instead, take some time to learn about your money. Consider it a challenge. Read books, listen to podcasts, find a great financial planner, and plan your future judiciously. Then, if you meet someone new, yours can be a relationship that you want to pursue, not one you think you have to maintain.

Megan: Holding two jobs is hard, but I'd rather work than count on someone else to bail me out.

Jessica: I love this chapter. I always knew I could make it on my own if that's what I want. So many people try to convince me I need to be in a relationship.

Kim: My friend Meg is a single mom. Her husband is always lavishing gifts on the kids. Some day they will understand, but right now it's so hard on her. She just doesn't have as much money.

Sharon: When your spouse dies, you feel like your world has ended. I got through it, but I know some women who never felt they could create a new life. Honestly, a few of them haven't.

Next Steps

Whether you are single by choice or suddenly find yourself single again, you can do this. You may need to learn some new skills, and it may take some time, but you will be able to function. Jot down some notes on what you should address first.

Prospering in the Workplace

Madam CJ Walker: First Black Woman Millionaire

SARAH BREEDLOVE WAS the first of her parents' children born out of slavery in Louisiana in 1867. However, her childhood was still difficult. Her mother died when she was seven, and her father died shortly afterward. She went to work as a domestic servant after having only three months of formal education.

Sarah married at the age of fourteen and had a daughter. She was widowed by twenty and made barely enough money to live by working as a laundress and a cook. She wanted a better life. By 1904, she was selling Annie Malone's African American hair care, her interest partly a result of her own scalp disorder. She then created her own product line.

Sarah had married Charles Joseph Walker in 1906 and became known as Madam CJ Walker. She used her name as the name of the business, and soon Madam CJ Walker's hair products were a huge national success. She even promoted her hair care process in Latin America and the Caribbean. During the nineteen-teens, the company claimed to have trained 20,000 women as sales representatives.

By 1917, the education wasn't just in product sales. She

also taught Black women financial skills and how to build businesses. She created state and local clubs for her employees and held a national conference for them in 1917. She rewarded not only top saleswomen but also those who made the largest donations to their local charities.

One of her most favorite quotes inspired not only her employees but entrepreneurs today: "Don't sit down and wait for the opportunities to come. Get up and make them."

Madam CJ Walker died in 1919 with an estate worth about $8,000,000 in today's dollars. This made her the wealthiest African American woman in the United States at that time. Her fortune was in addition to her philanthropic work. She established scholarships for women at the Tuskegee Institute and donated to the NAACP and black YMCA. Her daughter took over her company and continued its success. Even today, you can purchase products from the Madam CJ Walker brand.

Chapter 38

Creating a Resume

When her spouse received a promotion, she was excited, even though the new position meant they would have to move across the country. She really didn't like her current job and had wanted an incentive to make a change. The only parts of the transition she dreaded were packing and writing a new resume.

LIFE CHANGES OFTEN LEAD to the need for a new resume. Maybe you're looking for a new job, or perhaps you're applying for a competitive raise that requires the document. Although the resume writing process has changed over the years, the new formats aren't as confusing as some claim. With a little thought and time, you can show your accomplishments and skills in the best light.

The basics of a resume include your education, professional credentials, work experience, and accomplishments. It's highly unlikely you would want to include everything you've ever done. You want to organize your resume around the job you are seeking. In fact, if you are looking at multiple employers and positions, you may want to tweak your resume in a different way for each application. As a general rule, only include work experience and accomplishments that are relatively recent. Some experts suggest going back fifteen years, but I would modify this. If you have something impressive in your earlier days, by all means put it in. Additionally, your profession may have some specific information that needs to be included. Don't forget to check for resume writing tips specific to your field.

By focusing your resume, you will automatically shorten it. Try to keep the length at one to two pages. Any more than that may lose people's attention. Although I've seen the recommendation that a resume must be one page, you shouldn't omit important accomplishments and credentials just to achieve that length.

Whatever your background, never lie or exaggerate in your resume. Not having one specific skill is less likely to cost you the job than your employer discovering you made up accomplishments. Instead, if you believe you can do the job, include how your background makes you the perfect candidate.

As you are drafting your resume, don't use flowery language or overwrite to make your background sound impressive. Instead, write in clear, powerful words. Talk about not only your job title but what it requires that you do. As you read your new job's description, try to tie your experience to the needed skills. Write using powerful verbs. Avoid "to be" verbs when possible. For example, you might want to write "I possess" rather than "I am." Also, include up-to-date industry jargon and tone that shows you are knowledgeable.

Further, choose one traditional type of font, keep your paper in "portrait" orientation, and leave reasonable margins. Many potential employers who are reviewing your resume likely still print documents, especially if they are comparing them.

Additionally, proofread your resume for content, grammar, spelling, and punctuation. Be sure to stay consistent in your style. For example, if you are capitalizing every word or adding a period at the end of the description, do it every time. Once you have proofread your resume, do it again! Finally, give it to a friend for a final look. It's hard to see your own mistakes, and fresh eyes will find errors you won't believe you missed.

Finally, update all your social media platforms to reflect your updated resume. LinkedIn is particularly important, but you may need to review other sites as well. If you have your own website, be sure that how you describe yourself and your skills there matches your new resume.

Your potential employer may receive hundreds of resumes that look similar to yours. Take the time to create a portrait of yourself that captures the reviewer's attention, and put yourself on the short list.

∽

Megan: I don't have as many accomplishments on my resume as I wish. If I could earn my associate's degree, I think it would open doors for me.

Jessica: I don't have a long work history, but I still didn't include some of my early part-time jobs in my most recent resume. They have nothing to do with my college degree.

Kim: Sam had to interview a number of people for a position in her office. She was amazed how many applicants had typos in their submissions.

> Sharon: Sometimes, I think it's easy to lose the content in the formatting. Today, everybody looks like an expert if they can create a snazzy PowerPoint file.

Next Steps

Begin by reviewing your most recent resume. Brainstorm new accomplishments and, possibly, older credits you forgot to include. Then review any tips specific to your profession. Jot down some notes on the following lines to refresh your memory.

Chapter 39

How to Ask for a Raise

She knew how much she added to the firm. She wanted to ask for a raise but needed to time her request carefully. She decided to wait a couple of weeks until some external contractors wrapped up their work. Then, her boss would have enough time to listen to her ideas.

WHEN YOU HAVE A GOOD-PAYING JOB, that shouldn't be the end of the story. You also should feel confident asking for a raise if you believe you deserve one. But asking for a raise is scary. How should you approach it? What do you say? When is it appropriate? Address these concerns before you talk to your supervisor, but don't doubt yourself too much. You can't receive a raise if you don't request one. However, following several tips might make you more successful.

First, do your research. How much money do other people in your position make? Be sure to consider the salary level in your field and geographical area. What someone would make in New York City or San Francisco might differ widely from an employee working in the Heartland.

In addition to the salary range, what responsibilities do

their jobs entail? If you discover that other people who have positions similar to yours have additional responsibilities, then ask your supervisor if you could add those tasks to what you are currently doing. I know; it seems counterintuitive. You want to ask for a raise, and I'm suggesting you do more work at your current salary. However, showing initiative will likely impress your supervisor. It will also put you in a better negotiating position when you do ask for the raise.

Next, plan the timing of your request. In a perfect world, you would ask for a raise shortly after you completed a major accomplishment, found an error, or otherwise made a useful contribution to your employer. If you can't plan your request around that, maybe you could bring it up shortly after a good performance review. You want to ask for money at the time your employer is aware of your value.

Set up a meeting with your supervisor to make the request; don't just stop him or her in the hall and casually ask for a raise. The more seriously you make the pitch, the more likely they will be to consider it. If it's appropriate, you might create some summaries of your performance. Don't expect an answer on the spot. It's likely your supervisor isn't in a position to be able to grant you the raise even if he or she wants to do it. Give them time to go to their boss and make your case.

In your meeting, be specific and watch your words. If you want a raise, have a specific number in mind. Explain to your supervisor why you believe this amount is appropriate. Regardless of how the meeting goes, never threaten or accuse your supervisor as you ask for what you believe you deserve. If you come across as angry or desperate, you will change your supervisor's focus from your talents to your personal situation. That doesn't mean you shouldn't present yourself as strong and confident. Finding the right tone can be difficult.

Also, there is a chance that your supervisor will say no

when you ask for the raise. In fact, it's likely. If your request is shot down, control your anger, and don't threaten to quit unless you are willing to do it. Instead, ask what you can do to improve your chances for advancement in the future.

You shouldn't expect a raise too soon after you are hired. Give it time. However, there is no guarantee of an annual raise either. Requesting a raise because you have been in a position for a certain period of time (like a year) isn't nearly as strong as requesting the raise because of the value of your service.

Finally, if you want a promotion, represent yourself in a manner that fits with the level you are requesting. Dress appropriately on the day of the meeting. You want to handle yourself in a way that the supervisor can see you in that role and want you there.

If you don't get the promotion, it is likely you will be given some reasons why. Often, it's through no fault of your own. Sometimes the business just can't afford it. If that's the case, then take some time to discuss a few job adjustments that you would like to have in your working conditions. Maybe you can't have a raise, but perhaps you could be allowed to come to work thirty minutes later or leave thirty minutes earlier, giving you more free time without your employer's cash flow being adjusted. Alternatively, the company might be willing to give you some additional paid time off. Maybe the employer would pay for you to attend training. You can achieve an improvement in your working conditions without getting any cash.

If your supervisor explains that you aren't qualified for the raise or position you are requesting, ask her or him what you need to improve. See if she or he will help you create an action plan so you can achieve the level needed for the promotion. If the manager seems hesitant, don't push too hard. There may be other forces at work that you can't control.

Sometimes you don't get a raise for a reason that is altogether unfair. Certain environments make forward motion almost impossible. If that's where you find yourself, you might want to move to a different workplace. Hopefully, however, with a strategy and a little patience, you can advance in your current job.

Megan: I've been at our local diner for a couple of years. My position can't change, so I should ask for a raise since I've been a good employee.

Jessica: I haven't been in my position long enough for a raise. I'm going to save this chapter, though, and use it later when I make a request.

Kim: If I thought I could get a good raise from my current employer, I'd be less likely to want to form my own company. However, I've had several situations when better positions went to friends of the owners. That's just not fair.

Sharon: When I was first in the workplace, women were turned down for raises because the men needed the money more. The supervisors said the husbands had families to support. Ridiculous! Why do they think most of us were working back then? For the fun of it?

Next Steps

If you believe you deserve a raise, take some time to organize your reasoning and create a strategy for asking for the money. Jot your ideas on the following lines.

Chapter 40

Getting a Better Job

She wanted to apply for the new position. Unfortunately, she wasn't proficient at one of the required software programs. Her friend suggested she apply anyway. She didn't want to look arrogant, but she knew she had all the other skills. With some misgivings, she put in her application.

A RECENT STUDY showed a remarkable situation. When confronted with a job that had ten requirements, men would apply for the job if they had two of the skills, but women wouldn't apply unless they had eight or nine of them. Where men were certain they could learn on the job, women didn't give themselves the opportunity to be chosen because they didn't have all the skills and self-selected out first.

Would you like a better job? Do you need it because your cash flow is too tight? Or do you believe you have more to offer the world than your current position provides? If you said yes, read on!

The first step is to create or update your resume using the tips in Chapter Thirty-Eight. Remember, the competition is stiff these days!

Additionally, create a profile on LinkedIn or other professional networking sites. Keep your experiences up to date, and don't be afraid to reach out to establish a wide circle of contacts. Twitter and Facebook are nice, but for your professional reputation, you also need a LinkedIn profile.

Don't think of your social media profiles as static. You need to be involved. Read the posts of the people you follow. Make comments to these posts that show both interest and some knowledge of the field. If you don't have any knowledge about the article and it interests you, you might research the topic first so that your posts will be more relevant.

Additionally, you need to make posts yourself. It's okay to "lurk" on social media for a while if you aren't familiar or comfortable with a platform's format. You can go a long time simply responding to other people's ideas.

However, you want people to notice you. You need to read in your field, share articles, and offer opinions. Think of it as a process. First you read posts on the site, and based on those, you read other articles. You share those articles and begin to make comments. As you feel more confident and knowledgeable, your comments can become more detailed.

Eventually, you might want to write an article in your field. It's not as difficult as it appears. The biggest advantage to creating content is that doing so establishes you as an expert. I would prefer you create your own content rather than using a ghostwriter, even though it's common in some fields. Remember, if you don't create your content, your message won't be in your voice or necessarily represent you in an authentic way.

Establishing your voice can be difficult, especially if you're just starting to write. Your voice is your individualized tone. Do you want to be formal or conversational? Are you writing for peers or for people who need to understand your topic? In a world where everything can sound alike through industry jargon and artificial intelligence (AI), authenticity is important.

As a word of caution, remember that employers can find all your social media pages, not just your posts on business-oriented sites. All too often, I read about a celebrity or other noteworthy person who makes a thoughtless post or offers a suggestive picture on one of their social media platforms. A simple Googling of their name can bring up such posts. Remember that social media is forever, and it will haunt you if you make a bad mistake.

Once you have everything in order, don't be afraid to apply for positions. Both research and anecdotal evidence shows that women can be self-critical. Some of us don't think we are as good as our competition. Even if we secretly think we're great, we hate to say it out loud, especially if we are at a certain age or older.

For years, women were taught both overtly and in more subtle ways that nice girls don't promote themselves. In addition to this, we thought if we just did a good job, people would notice. I wish that were true. Unfortunately, when we quietly do excellent work, we often get ignored and people just come to expect it.

Additionally, women tend to volunteer to do tasks at work that don't lead to professional growth. For example, we may enjoy planning social gatherings, so we take that role on our office team. There's nothing wrong with that, but we should be careful to take on additional roles that will enhance our skills and get the boss' attention.

I had an experience like this myself. I was a new financial planner and joined a civic organization that began each meeting with a song. Because I play the piano, I began accompanying the song leader. I loved to do it, and everyone seemed to enjoy my playing. One day, someone asked me if I gave piano lessons. I said, "No. I'm a financial planner, and it takes most of my time." The person looked shocked. "Oh. I just assumed you were a musician." Once I made that discovery, I played the piano less and talked about my career more! I don't like people who always talk about their own accomplishments, but I took it too far the other way. Balance is everything.

Next, stretch yourself. If you are missing a critical skill that you need to accomplish your goals, don't be afraid to go back to school. A certificate or degree might seem unreachable, but I assure you that you can do it. Take some time to research the schools before you just enroll. Traditional universities offer online programs; you don't have to choose a for-profit institution. Also, look into how the school is credentialed because accreditation is important. Employers will probably take a little time to look at the source of your degree or certificate, and you don't want to obtain it from a diploma mill.

Once you have enrolled, double down or triple down and get through it. Any time you become discouraged, think how much you will love your new career. And if that isn't sufficient, think how much you will love the money you will earn! For more ideas on returning to school, review Chapter Twenty-Eight.

Getting a better job can sometimes be as challenging as getting any job. But with some planning and lots of hard work, you can do this. Believe in yourself and your abilities, and you will be surprised how far you can go!

◠

Megan: Okay—enough stalling. I'm going to call the community college and talk to an adviser.

Jessica: I have a friend who posts her entire life on a new social media platform. I keep warning her that it's not a good idea.

Kim: I'm active on social media, which helps me create business relationships. I've wanted my own firm for years, and I know I'll need to work hard to develop a client base.

Sharon: I've seen women sell themselves short. I hope younger women realize they should compete for any position they think they can hold.

Next Steps

Do you want a better job? What are some steps you should take to make it happen? Jot your ideas on the lines below.

_____

_____

_____

_____

Chapter 41

Determining Withholding

She always received a large tax refund. She knew she could do a closer estimate of what was due, but she used the refund to take her mom on a trip each year. Then, after a major change to the tax code, she was stunned when she received almost no refund at all. She knew her tax situation was complex, but she never expected not to benefit from the politician-promised tax cuts.

FOR MANY PEOPLE, the 2017 Tax Cuts and Jobs Act made little difference in their actual tax liability. However, if they were anticipating a refund after they filed, most were disappointed. The amount of withholding was adjusted by the government, causing some filers to experience larger paychecks, less tax withheld, and a smaller refund. Some actually owed taxes because they had other income sources that had no withholding. Had they reviewed and adjusted their W4, the IRS form that you complete to specify how much tax is withheld, they would have received the tax treatment they were anticipating. They may have a similar issue in 2026 if the tax brackets revert to their pre-Act, higher levels.

If you are like most people, you haven't looked at your W4 since you were hired or experienced a major life change, like a marriage or birth of a child. After you reviewed the form, you may have been bewildered. Most people didn't understand the concept of "allowances" and what they should select.

To help people withhold the correct amount of tax, the IRS revised the W4 in late 2020. The new form is much simpler, and the language in the five steps is clearer. Let's go over the process.

Step One is for your personal information, including your name, Social Security number, address, and filing status (single, married filing jointly, etc.).

Step Two applies if you work multiple jobs or if you are married and file jointly with your spouse. Here the IRS gives you three options, and you choose only one. Use their estimator and worksheets, or check the box to indicate if the two of you have only two jobs (one each), and earn similar salaries. Although you should consult your CPA before you choose which to select, I would recommend at least reviewing their estimator.

Step Three gives you the ability to adjust your withholding for the child and dependent tax credits. The simple fact is that you either are eligible for these credits, or you aren't.

Step Four allows you to make other changes. Maybe you receive income not subject to tax, or you anticipate deductions. You can lower your withholding for both of these situations. Further, you can choose to have additional tax withheld. This allows you some control over the amount of your refund. Remember, though, that a tax refund means you have given the government an interest-free loan of the overpayment.

Finally, Step Five is your signature.

Check out resources the IRS has provided to help you

with the changes to your W4. The link to the estimator in Step Two can be found here:

https://www.irs.gov/individuals/tax-withholding-estimator

If Step Two doesn't apply to you, you might still want to review the Paycheck Checkup page just to be sure you haven't forgotten something:

https://www.irs.gov/paycheck-checkup

By taking a little time to review your W4 now, you won't have a surprise when you file your taxes. Be proactive and understand what you are paying and what is being withheld.

Megan: I haven't had any issues with extra tax due, but I had a couple friends who work gigs in different fields. They always owe money to the IRS.

Jessica: Great. I just figured out what I should withhold, and they changed the rules!

Kim: We were expecting a larger refund than we received last year. I need to review my W4 or just anticipate a smaller refund.

Sharon: This chapter makes me happy that I am retired.

Next Steps

Take some time to review your W4. Ask your tax professional for any assistance you might need, and jot your notes on the following lines.

Chapter 42

Benefit Packages

When she was first eligible to enroll in her company's benefit package, no one explained how important her choices were. Or maybe they did, and she just didn't understand. A few years later, she wanted to purchase some plan-provided life insurance. She was surprised to learn she would need to qualify for the coverage. She thought she was included automatically.

When you're beginning a new job, the sheer process of joining a company can be overwhelming. You want to learn about your new responsibilities, and instead, you are filling out endless paperwork. Be careful as you make your selections. If you don't pay attention to your choices, it can cost you money in the long run.

Part of your paperwork might include enrolling in your company's benefit package (also called a "cafeteria plan" or "fringe benefits"). You should do research and be careful about rejecting an option. At the time you are first eligible for a company benefit, like insurance, if you enroll you are automatically covered. However, if you attempt to purchase the coverage later, you will probably be subject to underwriting.

This causes your personal health and circumstances to make a difference in what you can purchase and what the benefit(s) will cost.

Still, if you have a change in life circumstances and need an additional benefit, be sure to note your company's open enrollment period. During this time, you can modify your choices. It's usually once a year, during the fall.

Your benefits package can take different forms. Often, your employer will provide you with a certain amount of money and different benefits from which to choose. You have the option of keeping the money or purchasing coverage. Often, selecting the benefits provides you with a better deal than keeping the cash and investing it.

The most common benefit offered is health insurance. Thanks to the Affordable Care Act (aka "Obamacare,") health insurance is the one type of insurance coverage that isn't subject to underwriting at a later date. However, the coverage is important, and you still probably want to choose to purchase it as soon as you are eligible.

If you are married, you should compare the cost of any coverage available through your spouse as well as national coverage available in the Marketplace set up by the Affordable Care Act. If you have children, compare the cost of their coverage on all available policies and choose the one that offers the best benefits for the lowest cost.

Life insurance is also a common cafeteria plan offering. Your employer may offer a base policy with the option to purchase additional coverage. Sometimes, the cost is significantly less expensive than private coverage because it is a group plan. Life insurance can be subject to underwriting if you don't select an adequate amount initially and seek to increase your coverage later. Additionally, you may have the ability to purchase at least minimal coverage for your spouse.

Disability coverage is a third potential benefit. Disability insurance comes in two forms—short term and long term. Typically, employers include short-term disability coverage in a cafeteria plan, while long-term disability is usually a private purchase. Although you are more likely to use a short-term policy, long-term coverage helps avoid financial disaster if you were to become permanently disabled. Remember that when you pay the premiums on a disability policy, any benefit you subsequently receive is not subject to income tax. If your employer pays the premium, however, that benefit would be taxable. Disability policies typically only cover 60% of your salary, so losing additional money to taxation can be problematic.

Other kinds of coverage can be highly individualized, depending on the company. You may have the ability to fund a Health Savings Account (HSA), pay for childcare, or join a gym. Make your decisions based on the amount of money that is provided and the coverage that you need. You might talk to a financial planner to be sure you aren't overlooking something.

～

Megan: I just want a job where I can put this discussion to use.

Jessica: I was lucky that Human Resources explained how important my benefits decisions were. I enrolled in everything, so I won't have to deal with underwriting later unless for some reason I need considerably more life insurance.

Kim: I have a good friend who was diagnosed with cancer and was unable to work for almost a year. Her disability insurance kept her from financial ruin, although it was still tough.

Sharon: My husband purchased extra life insurance from his employer. His death was awful, but at least I stayed financially secure.

Next Steps

If you have a benefits package at your work, find out when you can adjust your selections or purchase additional coverage. Although you might have underwriting considerations, you should review your personal financial situation and see if you need to make any changes. Jot your notes on the following lines.

Chapter 43

Company Retirement Plans

She didn't remember enrolling in her company's 401(k) plan, and yet in December she received a statement. She owned an investment she was sure she hadn't chosen. She wasn't exactly upset, but she was confused.

JUST ONE OR two generations back, most people didn't invest in the stock market. If you were lucky enough to have a job with a pension, you didn't have to make investment decisions. That was managed by an external firm, and if you owned any stock, it was likely your employer's. Today, pension plans are rare. You are much more likely to have a retirement account in which you make most of the investment decisions. As a result, too many people become confused and don't participate in their company's plan.

Please don't make that mistake. As soon as you are eligible, enroll in your company's retirement plan and begin to make contributions. It's possible that your employer automatically enrolls you in the plan. If you choose not to participate, you must notify them, or your contribution happens by default. This is called a "negative election," and sometimes people discover, almost by accident, that they are enrolled in a retirement plan.

Although there's nothing wrong with this practice, it can be unnerving. To avoid surprises, learn everything you can about your company's retirement plan. Begin by taking some time to understand what kind of plan or plans your employer offers. Find out how much they are willing to contribute to your account. Does your employer provide a contribution automatically, or do they match your deferral up to a certain percentage?

It's important to participate in your company's plan at least up to the level of the employer match. If you don't, it's like giving up an automatic 100% return on your investment. For example, you defer 3%, they provide 3%, and suddenly 6% is being contributed into your account. However, just deferring 3% of your salary may not be sufficient to help you reach your retirement goal. Talk to a financial planner to see how much you should be setting aside.

The tax treatment of your retirement plan can be more complex than you might suspect. First, any money donated by your employer will always be in pretax dollars. The money you choose to defer might also be pretax and lower your current tax liability. Alternatively, you may be able to make a Roth election and fund your contributions in after tax dollars. This provides the advantage of no additional tax owed when you take distributions.

If you choose the Roth election, remember that this will cause you to have two separate retirement accounts—one pretax and a second after tax. There's no issue with this as long as you remember that you need to make investment decisions in both accounts.

What happens if you fail to make investment choices? Not too many years ago, the money would have stayed in a money market, an almost safe investment choice that typically earns a low return. Unfortunately, plan participants didn't always understand this, and near retirement discovered their accounts weren't worth nearly as much as they anticipated.

Of course, they should have been checking, and, of course, they should have been proactive. However, the Department of Labor decided to help out employees and create an automatic investment called a Qualified Default Investment Alternative (QDIA). QDIAs are most commonly target-date funds, but they can also take the form of a balanced fund or other moderate investment.

That's a lot of terms to understand, so let's look at each one. Target-date funds are common QDIAs, because they attempt to provide a return that potentially lowers risk as the owner nears retirement age. If your employer has chosen to use target-date funds for their QDIA, you are automatically enrolled in a plan with a date corresponding to your antici-pated retirement at sixty-five. If you are young, the fund will invest mostly in stocks. If you are near sixty-five, you will likely own more bonds.

Target-date funds were extremely popular when they were introduced but have come under more criticism recently. Their biggest flaws usually focus on how the fund managers choose to lower the risk over time. Some target-date managers keep investors more aggressive near retirement, while others take much of the risk off the table. The lack of continuity between funds can be confusing to investors.

Of course, the easy solution to understanding your target-date fund is to do some research. How aggressive is the fund when you are young? How conservative is it when you are older? How do the managers make this transition? You should be able to obtain all of this information from the investment company that is handling the plan.

Remember that you don't have to own the fund that corresponds to your potential retirement year. If you want to take some additional risk to potentially earn a better return, select a fund with a date later than the one you own. If you want to take less risk, select a fund with an earlier date. Of course, you can also choose completely different mutual funds to create your own asset allocation. You probably want to do this staying within the prescreened funds your plan suggests. That way you can tailor your portfolio to the risk level you choose. Just be sure you understand the risks and rewards of any investment you select.

Finally, your retirement plan may have a vesting schedule. This is a system where you must maintain employment for a certain period of time to receive all of your employer's contributions. Vesting can occur over time or all at once in a schedule explained in your plan document. Remember that any money you defer into the plan is always yours to roll out to a new employer or individual retirement account (IRA). The only money that might be lost would be that provided by your employer.

Your company's retirement plan is a critical tool for your future financial success. Invest some time to understand the details, then take advantage of the savings opportunity in a tax-advantaged situation. And once you've contributed to the plan, don't withdraw the funds early for other purposes unless you have a true financial disaster. It's a retirement plan, not a revolving door!

~

Megan: To participate in the plans at the companies where I work, I have to be full time.

Jessica: My employer matches my 401(k) contribution. I decided to select the Roth option, while their money was contributed in pretax dollars.

Kim: Our financial planner helped us decide how much to contribute to our retirement accounts, so we can stay on track. We also have a plan in case I branch out on my own.

Sharon: I worry that people think a 3% contribution and match will provide enough money for retirement. We had to contribute quite a bit more than that.

Next Steps

If you aren't participating in your company's retirement plan, consider enrolling. If your employer doesn't offer a plan, then save through an IRA or other investment account. Jot your notes on the following lines.

Chapter 44

Making the Decision to Retire

All around her, people were retiring. She and her colleague decided they would retire at approximately the same time. They worked collaboratively, and neither wanted to "break in" a new person. However, they weren't sure when they wanted to make the leap. They enjoyed both the work and the paycheck.

JUST THE OTHER DAY, I was in a group of people and heard someone ask, "When do you plan to retire?" I looked behind me to see who she was talking to, and much to my horror, she was looking at me! I'm fifty-seven, and I'm not interested in retiring. I'm not sure I've peaked yet!

And yet the question is common and trendy. The Financial Independence, Retire Early (more commonly called FIRE) movement might be an extreme strategy, but it seems as if many people just can't wait to stop working and live a life of leisure. Popular before COVID, the movement appears to have gathered steam, as some people really enjoyed the extended period of not going to the office. Be careful, though, because retiring early may not be as great as it sounds on paper.

First, if you want to retire, ask yourself why. Do you no longer want to work, or would you just like to feel appreciated in your job? If it's the latter, you might consider asking for a raise or applying for a different position. For tips on these skills, review those chapters earlier in this section.

Additionally, be careful that you have enough money in savings if you want to retire early. If you retire younger than sixty-five, the age when Medicare will most likely be available to you, you will need to have a plan for paying for your health insurance. This can be an expensive proposition, and it may take more resources than you had counted on spending.

Additionally, if you want to retire prior to age sixty-two, you are likely not yet eligible to receive Social Security payments. Even after age sixty-two, each year you don't take your Social Security benefit, it grows by 8% until you are seventy years old. To see the difference this makes, if your benefit were $1,000 a month when you are sixty-two and no other variables changed, it would be $1850.93 a month when you are seventy, eight years later! That much extra money might be worth the wait!

To be sure your savings are adequate for early retirement, you may want to break your cash flow analysis into three pieces. First, how much money will you need before you are eligible for Social Security and Medicare? Then, if you take Social Security, how much money will need until you receive Medicare? Finally, what is the amount you will need to meet any income deficit once you are eligible for both of these benefits? As you can see, the amount you will need decreases at each step. However, people are often shocked by how many of their resources they will use between fifty-five, a common early retirement age, and sixty-seven, a common Social Security full retirement age. Add to that the longevity women typically have, and you may find it is in your benefit to defer retirement for a few years.

If the financial math works and you no longer want to be part of the workforce, then ask yourself what you plan to do after you retire. Remember that many people define themselves by their jobs more than they realize. That's why it's not uncommon for someone to die shortly after retiring. If you want to retire, I want you to retire to something else—something new.

This new life doesn't need to involve earning money. Maybe you want to volunteer at the hospital, the library, or a local school. Perhaps you want to spend more time pursuing a hobby.

Some people dream of starting a business. If you're considering becoming an entrepreneur, you will want to do a careful cash flow analysis of your idea. Then, save enough to cover your business start-up costs. Although your enterprise may turn a profit in a year or two, you could need significant resources to reach that point. And many small businesses fail. I always worry when someone plans to start a business to increase their retirement income. The task can be challenging, and the outcome might not be as successful as you expect.

Additionally, people often don't realize that retirement can be lonely. Research shows that loneliness and lack of human interaction is a major cause of dementia. Don't fall into the trap of days alone, without contacting other people as we experienced during the COVID pandemic. Keep a social network that includes your friends from work. Then, find new outlets. Don't wait for someone to call you—call them and invite them out for lunch or coffee. If you have a faith practice, you might want to get more involved in activities there.

If you have grandchildren, then learn the technology they use to communicate. Get on the same social media where they post their activities. Learn how to make a video call on your phone. You can't expect them to write you a letter, but remember, a series of texts is an interactive letter where you can respond to each sentence. You don't want to spy on them, but they will likely love having you more in their lives, especially if you live long distances apart.

Retirement can be fun and rewarding, but it often isn't as wonderful as people anticipated. While you are still working, create some strategies for meaningful retirement activities. Then, when you decide to begin the next phase of your life, you'll have a plan.

> Megan: I don't think I'll ever have enough money to retire.

> Jessica: I can't imagine retiring yet. I'll reread this chapter later.

> Kim: I'm hoping that my consulting service can remain a part-time job, even while I'm in retirement. I like to work.

> Sharon: I've noticed that my friends who have clear plans for what they will do after retirement are happier. Not working sounds great, but it can be depressing and disorienting unless you have other goals.

Next Steps

Do you want to retire early? Do you want to work until you are older than seventy? Whatever you want, be sure you create a financial plan. What steps should you take as you think about retiring? Jot your notes on the following lines.

Chapter 45

Keeping Financial Stability

She couldn't take it anymore. Over the phone, her supervisor had just told her that if he said mushrooms had pink polka dots, then they had pink polka dots. This ridiculous statement was the result of her pushing back against a change in the program she supervised. He saw the change as expedient; she saw it as a potential lawsuit. As she got off the phone, she told him at least she knew what she had to do. Then she went to the rest of her team and told them she would be gone in two weeks.

SOMETIMES, quitting a job can feel like a moral imperative. Other times, we know we need to leave because the hours are cutting into our time with our kids. Or the stress is ruining our relationships.

Resigning from a job is scary because the financial implications are always extreme. How will we pay our bills until we find another job?

We talked about creating an emergency fund in the first section of this book. Remember, we discussed laying aside two weeks' worth of your bills and then continuing to save until you have a larger nest egg.

Generally, emergency funds are recommended in case you get fired. However, I believe they have a more powerful use than this. We already discussed how money in savings could help you avoid credit card debt. This chapter is focused on my third and final reason for recommending an emergency fund: it can provide you with options.

Whether we like it or not, having money gives us power because it provides us with options. Until now, we haven't talked about workplace harassment, because my overall focus in this book is your money. However, I know harassment exists, and it's a tremendous problem for many employees. Bosses can be anything from overtly obnoxious to subtly demeaning.

Co-workers can also make you miserable. A colleague once told me outright that I added nothing to the firm. In that same office, another male colleague gave me wrong information. After I caught it, I confronted him. He told me I should have known better. A third colleague refused to complete his half of the report we were writing. All of them made it clear they believed men were superior to women, who belonged in the home taking care of the kids. Three strikes, and I was out. I quit.

I was able to quit because I had access to enough resources. However, this happened many years ago, and the money was tight for a while. Had I previously saved six months' worth of my expenses, the transition would have been easier.

Create an emergency fund because it is empowering. When you save money because you are afraid you might be fired, you're diminishing your own worth. Of course, it can happen. However, you might want to find a better job—a job with more financial potential or room for advancement. Now you're saving money from a position of strength. Your actions move you from the mindset of being "acted on" to being the "actor." From this vantage point, it's much easier to prosper.

Megan: It will take me a while to save two weeks of my pay, but I love the idea of how it gives me power. I'm all about feeling empowered.

Jessica: I've been lucky, but my friend gets harassed at work all the time. I wouldn't be able to continue working in that environment.

Kim: I had a supervisor once who harassed me by nitpicking everything I did. I would follow his recommendations, and then he wouldn't like them. Years later, I found out he was suffering from mental illness.

Sharon: I can't tell you how many times I've seen friends keep jobs even though they were miserable. They didn't have any money saved, and they didn't have a choice.

Next Steps

Review the emergency fund information you collected in the first section of the book. Jot some notes on ways you could increase your savings level.

Living a Prosperous Life

Mabel Lee: Chinese Suffragette

MABEL PINGHUA LEE was born in Guangzhou, China, in 1896. She learned English in a missionary school, and by 1905 she was living in New York City because her father was a missionary to the United States serving as the Baptist minister of Morning Star Mission.

Even when she was very young, Mabel believed that feminism was the extension of democracy and equality to women. At the age of sixteen, Mabel led a women's suffragist parade in New York City on the back of a horse. Up to 10,000 people attended, and Mabel became a celebrity who worked tirelessly for women's rights. She wrote essays, gave speeches, and led additional events.

Ironically, in 1917 when women were granted the vote in the state of New York, Mabel was still denied the right she had fought so hard to achieve. The Chinese Exclusion Act barred Chinese immigrants from obtaining American citizenship. The Act wasn't repealed until 1943. Nevertheless, Mabel fought for women's rights, even though she would not be able to participate in them.

Instead, after graduating with a master's degree from

Barnard, she entered Columbia University to earn a doctorate in economics. She graduated in 1921 or 1922 as the first woman to earn a PhD from the university.

In 1924 Mabel's father died, and she became head of his mission in Chinatown, making it a haven for members who were shunned in other settings. She expanded the footprint to include a Chinese Christian Center, where English classes, medical services, and a kindergarten were available. She believed that Chinese churches should stay independent from their American counterparts. Although she died in 1966, her church still exists today and supports community civil rights.

Chapter 46

Financial Ratios

She wanted to own a house, but she wasn't sure it was a good idea. Her parents had always been financially shaky, and she didn't want to get in over her head. She needed to know how much she could afford to borrow.

IT CAN BE tricky to know whether or not you have enough money. You need to use numbers that haven't been created with the agenda of selling you something. You may also be afraid to ask your financial planner because you don't want condemnation. Some of the best tools you can use to determine your financial health are personal financial ratios. These measurements give you the opportunity to see how closely your financial situation resembles the benchmarks recommended by finance textbooks.

Don't stop reading here! You may be thinking to yourself, "OMG, Peggy, I don't want to solve math problems created by academics!"

I understand. I'm not going to drown you in jargon. Not only that, but you've also made it to Chapter Forty-Six—you can do this, and I'm going to make it easy.

We're going to look at three kinds of ratios. They measure how much money you need to have on hand, how much debt is usually safe to carry, and how to look at the kinds of debt you have.

To make these ratios a little more real, I would like to introduce you to Alicia. Alicia is young and ambitious. She lives in a fly-over state, so her salary isn't as high as if she lived on one of the coasts. On the other hand, neither are her bills. Still, she knows her cash is tighter than she wished it were. She has some money saved in her 401(k), and she inherited some stocks when her great aunt died. She has worked very hard to save her emergency fund. Alicia wants to buy a condo, but right now she rents. Here's Alicia's information:

What it's Called	What It Is	Cost
Gross Monthly Income	All the money she makes each month	$5,000
Net Monthly Income	Gross minus taxes and withheld benefits	$4,000
Liquid Savings	Money in the bank	$12,000
Total Assets	Car, investment and bank accts	$60,000
Total Long-Term Debt	Car payment, student loans	$50,000
Total Net Worth	Assets minus debt	$10,000
Monthly Housing	Rent, car payment, utilities, etc.	$39,600
Monthly Bills	Annual bills (above) divided by twelve	$3,300
Monthly Long-Term Debt	Cost of making a payment on the debt	$800
Monthly Consumer Debt	Credit cards and Car Payment	$500
Monthly Housing	Rent	$1,500

Now that we have her information, let's look at Alicia's ratios.

Emergency Fund Ratio

Formula: Liquid Savings/Annual Financial Obligations

AKA How Many Months of Expenses Can You Pay with Liquid Assets?

The emergency fund ratio focuses on liquidity, which is defined as the ease of turning an asset into cash without any loss of value. Usually, these assets are comprised of cash or money market accounts.

The ratio shows your ability to pay your bills if you suffer an income disruption. It compares the amount of your liquid savings to your annual nondiscretionary expenses. Remember that we calculated your nondiscretionary bills back in Chapter One.

I know you may have seen many recommended amounts for an emergency fund, but it averages from three to nine months of expenses. As we discussed earlier, the appropriate number for you depends on several things, including the stability of your employment or cash flow and your expectation of the likelihood of an income disruption. However, don't get too lulled into a sense of security. We call them emergencies for a reason!

Alicia's Emergency fund ratio is $12,000/$39,600 or almost four months' worth of bills. Although she could save more, she is above the minimum hurdle. Way to go, Alicia!

Total Debt to Net Worth Ratio

Formula: Total Debt/Net Worth

AKA How Much Debt Do You Have Compared to Your Net Worth?

This ratio shows how much debt you have as a percentage of your net worth. Remember that the basic definition of your net worth is your assets minus your liabilities. If your net worth is negative, which isn't that uncommon when you are young, then this ratio will be depressing, but don't despair. You likely will have more assets and less debt as you get older, so this ratio should improve by getting smaller over time. Complete the calculation once a year to help you track your progress.

Alicia's total debt/net worth ratio is $50,000/$10,000, or five. As she pays off her student loans and automobile, this number will get smaller as the debt declines and the net worth improves. Even though research shows that her college education will likely help her obtain a higher-paying job, her current student loan debt is a drag on her finances. Even though her automobile has a loan against it, it has a little cash value above that.

Long-Term Debt to Net Worth

Formula: Long-Term Debt/Net Worth

AKA How Much Long-Term Debt Do You Have Compared to Your Net Worth?

Another debt ratio separates long-term debt from total debt. Long-term debt is limited to liabilities that will be paid longer than the course of one year. This debt is often viewed as better debt than short-term debt, because it is comprised of loans on assets, while short-term debt is usually consumer debt, such as credit cards. Like the total debt to net worth ratio, your long-term debt to net worth ratio should also improve (get smaller) as you get older. Once your mortgage is paid off, your long-term debt to net worth ratio might be quite low—that's a good thing!

Most of Alicia's debt is long-term, except for her credit card balances. Once she buys a condo, the ratio may get even worse as her amount of long-term debt will rise substantially.

Consumer Debt Ratio

Formula: Consumer Debt/Net Monthly Income

AKA How much Credit Card and Car Payment Debt Do You Have Compared to Your Net Income?

The consumer debt ratio is a debt analysis ratio. Consumer debt payments can rapidly lead to financial instability. This ratio compares your monthly consumer debt payments to net (after tax) monthly income. The goal is to have the ratio less than or equal to 20%. If you pay your cards off each month, you can ignore this ratio, even if you have a balance on the card at the time you're reading this chapter.

Alicia pays $500 a month on her credit cards and car payment. Since her net monthly income is $4,000, her ratio is 12.5%, so she is in good shape on her consumer debt ratio, although I'd advise her to try to pay her cards off when she can to avoid the higher interest.

Monthly Housing Costs to Gross Income Ratio

Formula: Monthly Housing Costs (Rent or PITI)/Monthly Gross Income

AKA What percent of your income are you paying on your total housing costs?

Owning a home is a common goal, but we are often uncertain what we can afford to purchase. This ratio has you calculate monthly housing costs, either rent or mortgage principle, interest, taxes, and insurance (PITI), divided by gross monthly income. Gross monthly income is your income before you have taxes and benefits withheld. The goal is to have this ratio less than or equal to 28%.

If you want to figure out how much home you can afford, you can solve a version of this formula:

Gross (pretax) monthly salary x 28% (.28) = maximum monthly payment including PITI.

Once you know what's possible, you won't be disappointed by looking at something and then discovering that you can't afford it. Notice that I didn't say qualify for it. Typically, you can qualify for home mortgage payments higher than this percentage. However, if you keep the payments to 28% of your gross income, you will be more financially successful.

Alicia's rent is $1500, and her gross income is $5,000. This makes her housing ratio 30%. Although that's higher than the 28% that is recommended, she's close. I don't think she needs to move; however, she shouldn't consider upgrading until she is more financially secure.

Monthly Housing Costs and Other Debts to Monthly Gross Income

Formula: Housing Costs + Other Monthly Debt Payments/Monthly Gross Income

AKA What Percentage of Your Income Is Used for Debt Payments?

The final debt analysis ratio in this chapter looks at all your monthly payments together. Your housing costs (PITI) and other monthly debt payments divided by your gross income should be less than or equal to 36%. As you pay off debt, this ratio should improve.

Alicia's total debt is $2,800 ($1,500 + $500 +$800), and her gross income is $5,000. As a result, her total debt ratio is 56%. That is significantly higher than the recommended ratio, but she doesn't have many options. She needs a car, and she chose a used one with a good safety record. Her major crisis here are her student loans.

She should try to pay down her debt as quickly as she can, taking loan forgiveness legislation into consideration. She might take any money she is still saving for her emergency fund and apply half of it to her debt.

Now that we've looked at Alicia, it's time for you to complete your own review. If your financial ratios are all within these guidelines, you are probably in great shape! Congratulations! However, what if they're not? What do you do if you have numbers not within the recommendations? First of all, don't beat yourself up. This is a judgment-free chapter. Financial instability occurs, sometimes for people you wouldn't expect. If you aren't where you want to be financially, at least you know where you are.

Remember your financial plan is a long game. Good scores on these ratios can take years to achieve. As a result, your best strategy is to calculate each of them once a year (or before you make a major purchase). Keep your information somewhere easy for you to find, and create a comparison chart of where you are year over year. Begin by trying simply to improve each measurement every year.

The problem with comparing yourself to the goal percentages occurs when you are quite a distance from where you want to be. I've seen people realize that their debt is significant. Rather than purchasing less, they buy more because they believe there can never be improvement. Don't do that. You should be proud of yourself for completing this exercise. Many people are so afraid of their money that they won't look at their debt level.

Megan: Even though I won't like the numbers, I need to run these ratios. I can't fix something if I don't know it's broken. Like Peggy said at the beginning of the book, I need to be brave.

Jessica: I love knowing how much of my paycheck I should be spending on a mortgage. I don't want to get in over my head.

Kim: I'm always surprised how well salespeople can convince you that you can afford something. Running the numbers before I make a purchase just makes sense to me.

Sharon: I know that little in my financial life is truly black and white, but I like having specific numeric ratios to use for goals.

Next Steps

Insert your own financial data into these ratios and check your results. What's going well, and what needs a little work? Jot your ideas on the following lines.

Chapter 47

Stay Informed and Take Action

She watched the news every night and was amazed how that simple activity changed over the last fifty years. Thirty-minute daily summaries had turned into never-ending hours of commentary on networks, cable, and social media. She wondered if the extra coverage was leading to useful additional information or just spin and hype. A child of the 'sixties, she tried to stay informed, but it was difficult.

Do you try to keep up with legislative issues that are important to you? Do you review upcoming bills on your state's and nation's stage? If you don't, you're in good company. Many people find the details of their daily lives consuming all their time. Big issues seem to pass us by. But that may be changing, and it's never been more important.

Recent civic gatherings harken back to an earlier time when people focused on effecting change. In fact, social concern may be one of the greatest outcomes of the early twenty-first century. People, especially women, appear to have remembered that democracy is hard work. To keep the

305

liberties they want to have, they have to stay aware of them and take vocal positions to keep them safe.

Today, more than ever, you should choose several issues you value and get involved. You might work on the local, state, or national level, depending on the cause. Whatever your passion, remember you can make a difference.

Along with your own legislative concerns, I also want you to pay attention to financial bills that are proposed. Consider the potential impact of suggested legislation, and keep an eye on changes to the tax code!

I know you have a million things to do, but staying aware of financial legislation doesn't need to take all your time. Just half an hour a week—maybe less—can keep you informed. And staying informed can help you stay safe.

One particular issue to follow is the duties owed to you by your financial professional. Some advisers have the legal responsibility to act as your fiduciary. Others have a "best interest" standard that has recently been adopted. Securities and Exchange Commission regulators go to great detail to explain that this is not a fiduciary level of care; it's lower. However, they are unclear about the details, and the issue is a mess. Over time, I'm hoping for clarification, but for now, you need to question financial professionals before you are willing to work with them. You might want to review what I discussed in Chapter Twelve. If the regulations won't protect you, you need to protect yourself.

A second area where you should stay informed is the issue of financial exploitation of seniors. Legislation meant to protect the elderly is being formalized all across the United States. Most of us have older people in our lives whose financial security is our concern and responsibility. Keep up with how the law can assist you in helping them.

Finally, although there are many other financial issues you

will discover as you read, I encourage you to keep up with the tax code. Remember that the Tax Cuts and Jobs Act provision designed to benefit individuals is set to expire in 2025. Only the corporate rate reduction is permanent. As expiration of the individual income tax rates approaches, I expect legislators will want many adjustments and compromises. You should keep up with what these are. Of course, you should talk to your CPA and financial planner, but you should also try to keep up with the changes, yourself.

I understand that staying informed can be challenging, but I believe your effort is worth the time. Remember the popular saying, "If you're not at the table, you're probably on the menu."

Megan: I've never paid attention to politics. Everything today shows me why I need to stay up to date.

Jessica: I always vote, and I try to stay informed on the issues. I'm surprised how many of my friends don't watch the news. Neither do their parents.

Kim: I've been doing some reading about the liability owed to you by your financial adviser. The terminology has become confusing, and I hope something will clarify it.

Sharon: I have friends who have experienced financial exploitation. I'm glad the laws are being strengthened.

Next Steps

Take some time to read about the issues discussed in this chapter. Other concerns may be important to you as well. Create a strategy for staying informed on topics of interest to you. Jot some notes on the following lines.

Chapter 48

Avoiding Fraud

She tried to navigate the internet carefully. She kept protective software on her computer and changed her bank and shopping site passwords periodically. One day, while watching the news, she discovered that one of her financial institutions had been compromised. She wasn't sure what steps she should take.

AT LEAST ONCE A MONTH, we hear that another major corporation has been hacked. Banks, brokerage firms, retail stores, even credit reporting agencies—these days it seems like everyone is a potential victim. Millions of Americans are impacted every year.

The pattern is concerning and unsettling. Consumers' behaviors, for the most part, aren't causing these hacks, and they can do little to avoid them. Additionally, given the widespread nature of the breaches, it's almost impossible to avoid doing business with places where hacking occurs. However, I believe the most disturbing part of the events is the lack of explanation as to how they happened.

Often, the company's first announcements say they do not believe their data loss was the work of dangerous, sophisticated hackers. This does not give me confidence. I hate to think that amateurs could hack multi-million-dollar corporations and agencies, although it's possible.

Still, if you find yourself the victim of a data breach, you're probably more worried about how to fix it than what caused it. You can take several actions to help protect the privacy of your information. First, the organization should provide you with some strategies and maybe some free or reduced-cost services. Take any reasonable steps that they believe will best keep you safe.

Next, I recommend going to the Federal Trade Commission (FTC) website, https://www.identitytheft.gov. This comprehensive site provides strategies when multiple types of information are taken. For example, you need a different plan if your Social Security number is stolen than if someone has your driver's license information. Because it's a government site, the recommendations are designed to be objective—offering suggestions and not products for sale. Here are just a few of their ideas:

• If someone calls saying they are from the IRS, do not believe them, even if they have part of your Social Security number. Scams like this are designed to get the rest of your number when hackers only have some of the digits.

• If someone hacks an online password, of course change it, but also try to change your username.

• If your child has a credit report, it's likely someone has hacked his or her identity. Children can't apply for credit cards, borrow money, or complete transactions that would create a credit report.

Other tips exist on the site as well, including specific strategies for recent cases of identity theft. Check it from time to time to help you stay current.

Third, consider freezing your credit at the three major credit agencies: Experian, TransUnion, and Equifax. This can be done over the phone or online. There is a modest fee for this service. Additionally, write down all the details of your conversations with these agencies. At some point, you will want to turn off the credit freeze. For example, you might need an extension of credit for a purchase. To access your own credit, you must have all the information you provided to the freezing agency. For example, the time I froze my credit, I had to provide the service company with some identifying information. Make sure you keep track of the details—even writing it down in two or three places! You don't want to lose it.

Once you have put your identity safety plan in place, do not check your own credit score constantly. Some services claim they do not report personal credit checks, but most of the time, checking your credit negatively impacts your credit score.

Finally, file your taxes as early as possible. The hack may have accessed all of your personal information, including everything criminals would need to file a tax return in your name, change the address, and send themselves a refund. The IRS is aware of this weakness but has little it can do about it.

Discovering that your data has been hacked can be unsettling and scary. However, don't panic. By taking some steps, you can lessen the impact of this increasingly common crime.

Megan: Everyone I know completes nearly all their financial transactions online.

Jessica: I was part of a data breach once. Nothing happened, but it's scary.

Kim: I hate that I can't do anything to avoid being a victim of these hacks. What am I supposed to do? Stop shopping?

Sharon: I find it frustrating that after I do everything I can to keep things safe, these companies can't seem to stop the leaks.

Next Steps

It's worth your time to go to the FTC website and review the steps to take with different kinds of data loss. Then, if you have an issue, you will know what to address first. Jot your notes on the lines below.

Chapter 19

Financial Stress and Your Health

As she looked up from her laptop, she turned her head and heard her neck crack. Paying bills often left her with a headache. Juggling due dates and dollar amounts was so stressful. She sighed and went to the cupboard for a glass and a bottle of pain reliever.

You PROBABLY ALREADY KNOW THAT stress impacts your health. It can be as simple as the headache that doesn't want to go away and as dangerous as the auto-immune disease that arises from constant pressure.

Financial stress can be physically debilitating. We fret about finding work, advancing in our careers, paying our bills, and being seen as successful. Financial concerns aren't just issues for those with limited income. They know no economic boundaries.

We've spent nearly all of the book talking about financial issues and solutions. In this chapter, I want to remind you that you also need to take care of your physical self in order to prosper. I am not a physician or dietary specialist, so you should consult those professionals for medical and nutritional advice. Still, I want to review some common issues, because your health and your money are surprisingly related.

For starters, get enough sleep. Sleep is becoming a trendy topic, and research is starting to show its importance. Sadly, many of us still brag about how little sleep we need. But be careful. When we're sleep deprived, we don't think through our decisions as carefully. We tend to act quickly, and this can easily lead to overspending. It can also cause us to make other financial decisions that aren't necessarily in our long-term best interest.

Next, try to get enough exercise. Look for those activities you like to do. I hate to go to the gym, but I love taking care of my horses, Maggie and Oreo. With seventy-pound bales of hay, fifty-pound bags of feed, and large buckets of horse by product that I dump, I get a great workout several times a week. And I look forward to taking care of them! Find an activity you love. Just taking the dog for a walk several days a week is great. Physical activity lowers your stress and makes you stronger, which may improve your health.

Third, be careful of the rabbit hole of social media and popular culture. Although we know that online images are photoshopped, we tend to compare our bodies anyway. Body shaming leads to issues that impact health, well-being, and ultimately, our relationship with money.

Finally, watch your eating habits. Stress eating is so common it's often the punchline of a joke. And yet, when we eat because of stress, it seems we never crave broccoli! I would urge you to try to maintain a reasonable diet without participating in a lot of fads. Remember, just as financial success involves creating a plan that you can live with, eating habits also need to be reasonable. Set goals that you can obtain, and try to keep them. Cook at least several times a week to cut down on salt and fat. You'll save money too!

Good health has a strong financial impact. First, if your health is good, you aren't spending money on avoidable physical ailments. Next, being healthy allows you to work and earn money. Many people have limited earning potential because their health prohibits their working full time. Finally, healthy people tend to be happier, and that helps our prosperity.

Megan: I know that worrying about money costs me sleep.

Jessica: People don't show their real bodies on social media. Filters can take off a few pounds and erase wrinkles. Still, sometimes I feel like my body doesn't always measure up!

Kim: I hate to admit that I almost brag about how little I sleep. I'm super busy, I can't fall asleep early, and my alarm goes off by six a.m. Maybe I should make more of an effort to get rest.

Sharon: I'm so old I remember the grapefruit diet of the 1970s! Okay, I'll admit it. I tried eating that nasty stuff for a few days, but then I gave up. Now I see all the trends, laugh, and continue to eat a balanced diet.

Next Steps

Take time to schedule some stress-reducing activities. Maybe you want a massage. Perhaps you just need to go to the grocery store and pick up healthier foods. Jot your ideas on the following lines.

. . .

_____

_____

_____

_____

_____

_____

_____

_____

Chapter 50

Fear of Being a Bag Lady

Every time she went downtown, she checked her purse to be sure she had some one-dollar bills. She knew she probably shouldn't give money to the homeless, but the women broke her heart. They frightened her too. Well, not really them, but what they represented.

A RECENT SURVEY revealed women's top five financial concerns. Number three was becoming a bag lady. That felt extreme to me, even though the survey seemed reasonably conducted. So I started asking women—especially those over a certain age. It's important to note that none of them appeared to struggle financially, and all were currently living in homes they either owned or rented. However, I asked them anyway. Were they afraid of becoming a bag lady?

Much to my surprise, the most common answer was, "Of course, I do."

Wow. I didn't know what to say. I thought about their responses for a long time, and eventually the bag lady business began to make sense. I think the reasons for the participants' concerns were fairly complex. Accordingly, let's address a bigger issue in this chapter—financial fear.

Financial fear occurs for many different reasons. A major cause is the financial services industry itself. And the issue exists on many levels.

Financial service companies target women, and sometimes, their focus is designed to be empowering. Women need to realize that likely they will be responsible for managing their money at some point in their lives, if not for their lifetime. The good campaigns show these women that they can be financially successful. However, all too often, the information is designed to make women fearful.

The firms want you to work with them. If they were to convince you that you do pretty well managing your money on your own, why would you seek out their services? So be aware that you are seeing carefully crafted messages on television, in print, and in social media that are designed to get you through their doors.

Individual financial advisers may perpetuate the concept that you lack knowledge and power. In their offices, fearmongering can get worse. I know a woman who attended one of those awful "dinner and a PowerPoint" financial seminars. Remember my story in the earlier chapter about the adviser who warned women about eating cat food?

That practice is just wrong. Whether the women in that room had saved enough for retirement or not, terrifying them with the goal of selling a product was gross and unfair. How do you combat an adviser like that?

First, throw those invitations in the trash. Fortunately, they are less popular than they were a few years ago. However, remember "there is no such thing as a free lunch" or dinner. The giver wants something from you. The problem with the dinners is similar to "Hotel California"—

once you go in, it's difficult to get out before the pitch is over.

If you do opt for the free meal, do not sign up for a product that night. If you want to schedule an additional meeting to talk about what the speaker is selling, then by all means, sign up for a consultation. But don't make a purchase on the spot. Don't even buy anything on the initial visit to the office. Be sure the adviser is both someone you want to work with and that he or she is offering something you really want to own.

Never make decisions based on fear. Instead, if you are considering a new financial professional, ask yourself a few questions.

First, how does the adviser make you feel? Do they treat you like you are intelligent, regardless of your current level of financial knowledge? Regularly, new clients come to me, and explain that they thought their last adviser was just telling them not to worry their "pretty little heads" about those nasty finances. He, the adviser, would take care of everything. *Please.* Of course, you are considering hiring that person to help you take care of your financial affairs. But managing your assets should be a collaborative process, not something that occurs because the adviser suggests you can't do it. Unfortunately, you may begin to doubt your abilities to make decisions on your own behalf, and pretty soon, you may agree with him. But don't go there! That's toxic to your financial health.

One of the reasons I wrote this book, as I said in the introduction, was my aggravation with the way finance frequently presented to women. If you feel as though the financial adviser doesn't respect you, run away!

If you go to see your financial professional with your husband, does the adviser talk to you as much as to him? Sadly, for many women, the answer is often, "No." You don't want to work with someone who will focus all his attention on the man in the relationship. It creates a scenario where you feel like your opinions and contributions aren't as important. Additionally, if you ever need to work with this adviser on your own, you will be less likely to have the tools and knowledge necessary.

If you are single, have a partner, or a same-gender spouse, the advice of the last paragraph still holds. You want your financial adviser to talk about your concerns with you and treat you with respect.

I have included an entire chapter on the qualifications of an adviser, but here in our conversation about financial fear, I want to help you find a financial planner who gives you confidence.

Even if you are working with a financial professional you trust, to increase your confidence, you should take steps to understand whether or not you are financially okay.

First, check your level of debt using the ratios we calculated earlier. Sometimes people take extreme actions to manage their bills. I know it's popular to refinance your home to pay off consumer debt, but this can be risky. The way to avoid being a bag lady is to have a place to live. Don't take actions that will put your housing at risk unless you absolutely have to do so.

Remember, if you get in severe financial difficulty, you can discharge credit card debt in bankruptcy. In English, that means you can declare bankruptcy and get rid of your credit card debt. However, if you pay off your credit cards by stripping all of the equity from your house, you will increase your risk of losing your home.

Additionally, avoid using your house as a source of capital. Some financial advisers recommend that you take out a home equity loan for investments, reminding you that your projected return is higher than the interest you would pay on the mortgage. The problem with this mentality, outside of the fact that the adviser is likely earning a commission from the sale, is that projected returns are just that—projected. Virtually any investment can go down in value.

I know the rationale is that over time, markets go up. The problem is they might not go up during the time that you have extended your mortgage.

I have another concern as well. I've seen people talked into investing their home equity in a product that isn't remotely stable. Instead, it's something exotic sold with the suggestion that it will likely earn extremely high returns. Note the word, "likely."

At worst, these investments are fraudulent. At best, they are risky. Remember that you earn a return for taking risk. Any time an adviser assures you that you can anticipate a high return, if it's even legit and legal, it's risky.

Of course, the final decision is yours. Do you want to extend the mortgage on your home, possibly extending your payments into retirement when your cash flow might be more limited? Do you want to purchase an investment that's likely risky and has a good chance of going down in value before it goes up? Make sure you have all the information you need, and then you can make your own choices.

As the next step to help you control your financial fear, look at your retirement cash flow projections. Are you on track for having enough money? If you are, then everything is probably okay. If you are still uncertain, go back to Chapter Six and look at all variables.

Are you sure you have properly calculated your cash flow need? If not, run your numbers again. Don't forget to include your retirement healthcare and potential assisted living costs. Are your Social Security projected benefits still valid? You can confirm them by looking online or at your most recent Social Security statement.

Have your rate of investment return assumptions been met? In other words, if you are assuming a 7% portfolio return, have you been achieving it? Is inflation running according to your assumption? Are you saving as much as you anticipated? Has anything changed in your life that reduces your ability to work?

I know those are a lot of questions. But here's the thing. If you can answer each question positively and nothing has derailed your plan, you can be pretty confident you won't become a bag lady.

Even after you've determined your financial planner is acting as your fiduciary, reviewed your debt level, and calculated your financial need, and you know you are on course, are you still fearful of running out of money? Then you need to consider the origin of your fear.

We've looked at the fields of behavioral and interior finance in other parts of this book. They apply here, as well, particularly the field of interior finance. We talked originally about money scripts in Chapter Thirty-Three.

Remember that money scripts are the phrases we have heard about money since we were young. Most money scripts come from our parents, but sometimes they come from teachers, ministers, or friends' families. These money scripts are usually declarative sentences like: "You can't trust people who have a lot of money." Or "To get ahead, you have to work hard all the time."

The problem with a money script is it embeds into us, and it shapes our behavior. Most insidiously, we often don't know we are altered by it. Money scripts can be anything, but they are often critical or judgmental voices.

When you buy into a money script, although you want

financial stability, subconsciously you may be fighting the concept that having wealth is bad. Alternatively, if you are frightened of financial insecurity, and you have taken the time to understand your investments, it may be that from an early age you were told that you can't trust the stock market. If you still have "Depression Era" family members offering input, this is not only possible but probable.

Fighting a money script can be tricky. The first step is to recognize it. What money sayings do you remember from your childhood? What sort of influence could these have on your current financial situation? What steps could you take to adjust your beliefs into something that will be less stressful and more productive?

Interior finance issues, like money scripts, are different from most of the components of behavioral finance. Interior finance focuses on your personal experiences. Behavioral finance tends to look at irrational investing behavior within large groups of people. Logical fallacies, similar to those you may have studied in other disciplines, have financial implications in behavioral finance. For example, if you are worried about the stock market, you may be focusing only on those bad periods of the market that are prevalent in people's minds. Looking at a larger frame, or a longer time horizon, can show you that those declines, although bad, are part of a long-term upward movement. Understanding this concept may help you be less afraid, especially if you have already worked with your financial planner to put together an investment portfolio within your risk tolerance level.

Additionally, we tend to focus on specific events—and those are usually bad! At the time of the writing of this book, we're twenty years past the dot.com financial bubble of 2000-2003. However, I still have clients who don't want to invest in technology because of what happened then. They are uneasy, even when I show them the overall performance of this sector. Their behavior shows how easy it is to remember bad events and ignore data that contradicts memories.

I can't promise that you will always feel extremely confident about your finances. However, you shouldn't live fearfully. By implementing some of the ideas in this chapter, I hope you will be less afraid of becoming a bag lady. That will free you to focus on those parts of your life that make you prosperous.

Megan: Maybe I worry too much about how Charlotte and I would survive if I lost one of my jobs. I have options with family and friends if it all goes wrong.

Jessica: I'm offended when professionals are condescending to me. Not only am I a woman, but I'm also young. I hate it when people assume I'm uninformed.

Kim: I've never thought I would be a bag lady, but I have wondered if I would ever be able to retire. I'm hoping now I know enough to find the answer to that question.

Sharon: I can relate to the fear of being a bag lady. I think people are afraid of what they don't know, and I'm believe many of my friends don't understand their money.

Next Steps

Are you afraid you might end up being a bag lady? If so, follow the steps in this chapter and look again at any other chapters that address your concerns. Jot your ideas on the following lines.

_____

_____

_____

_____

_____

_____

_____

_____

_____

Chapter 51

Trustworthy Information

She didn't know how they got her contact information. She regularly received emails promising double-digit investment returns. Flyers came in the mail. She had never heard of the investment firms, the companies they wanted her to purchase, or the "experts" who touted their valuations. She deleted them and threw them away.

DECIDING whether or not something is "fake news" seems to be the question for the moment, whether you're talking about politics, celebrity behavior, or financial advertising. Sometimes telling the difference between the real and the fake is particularly important, especially when you are trying to understand your investments. Although financial information is plentiful, it's hard to tell the difference between research, advertising, and hype. Fortunately, you can take some steps to becoming a savvy consumer.

Begin by checking the credentials of the person who wrote the article. Today, with online publishing, it's easy to look like an expert. Because of this, before you trust what the article says, do some research. Just because an author has a list of letters after his or her name doesn't mean they're someone you should trust. Take some time to learn what the different acronyms mean. Maybe the authors are real experts, but maybe they aren't.

Additionally, if a financial professional provides you with a document that they call research, see who financed the work and where it was published. Today, research occurs outside university settings, and public/private partnerships are getting popular. In fact, some commercial firms have a reputation for creating great data. Still, sponsors may have an interest in the outcome and may present the findings in a way to make themselves look good. If the research has been completed by the same company offering the product, look for other resources that present information on the topic. Smart financial planning should include more than one source on a product or subject.

Another way to tell the difference between research and advertising is by looking at the conclusions. Typically, research offers findings or results, while advertising promotes specific products. For example, research might discuss the performance of a stock market index, like the S&P 500, while advertising might offer data but would eventually mention a specific S&P 500 mutual fund. Both conclusions might still be accurate and compelling. However, if the blog, article, or podcast ends with a specific fund recommendation, you have been listening to an advertisement.

If you have determined that what you are reading is meant to persuade you to make a purchase, look at the results carefully. If the piece touts investment performance, two components are particularly important. First, check to see how the investment returns compare to the appropriate market index. You may need to do a little more research into the fund to determine the most appropriate comparison. If the fund holds international stocks, you wouldn't want to compare it to the US stock market. Instead, you would want to use an international index.

Next, remember that investment performance varies over time. Look at any performance results that the document provides and compare them to equivalent market index results over the same period of time. Cherry picking timelines can mislead you on investment returns.

Hidden costs can also make an investment less compelling, and they are often omitted from advertising material or buried deep in the fine print. What commission and fees occur at the time of the purchase, and what annual expense ratios will you need to pay? Is there a surrender period? Remember that surrender periods limit your access to some or all of the funds invested. You might be able to take a small distribution during each year of the surrender period, but if you want to take it all, you pay a penalty.

Further, are investment returns provided gross (before) or net (after) of fees? You want to know what expenses and costs will lower your potential profit. Remember that all investments cost something. You are looking for reasonable fees and transparency.

Finally, as I said earlier, don't be in a hurry. Most advertising is crafted to compel you into taking immediate action. Presenters or salespeople will strongly encourage you to sign up now. Don't do it. Take the material, go home, and do your own research. You can always say "yes" tomorrow.

With social media, "advertorials," and impressive materials, distinguishing between research and advertising can be difficult. However, if you do a little work and take your time, the process will be easier. You want to make good decisions based on accurate information.

> Megan: I don't understand investing well. I've always thought promises of high rates of return were good. I guess they really aren't.

> Jessica: I don't want to be critical of my mom, but I feel like I understand online sources better than she does. Just because it's on a website doesn't make it true.

> Kim: I know that sometimes research is persuasive, but most ads I read are more to generate sales out of a veneer of information. It's confusing.

> Sharon: I get invitations to financial seminars nearly every week. They all go in the trash.

Next Steps

Be careful not to confuse advertising with research. Before you make any decisions to purchase investments, or for that matter any other expensive item, take some time to look over the facts, the costs, and any fees or interest. Jot your notes on the lines below.

_____

_____

_____

Chapter 52

Prosperity Is More Than Money

She was a whiz in college and soon after graduating landed a career in her profession. She joined the civic organizations in her town. By all external standards, she was stunningly successful. However, she wasn't happy. She had always wanted a different career and more home life. How could she break out of all this and create the life she wanted?

FOR TWENTY YEARS, I've tried to help people become prosperous. That's always my focus, whether in my writing or financial planning practice. I provide people with financial knowledge and skills that they can use to create a life that brings them joy.

I think "prosperity" is an interesting word. I began to use it years ago, soon after I entered the field of finance. Then, I was told I needed an "elevator pitch," a brief way of describing what I did. People in the business told me that an elevator pitch would help me create my "brand." A brand? Not only did I not have a brand, but I also didn't even have clients!

Still, I set out to create a brief way of describing what I

did. I have never liked the word "rich." It's problematic for several reasons. First, to me it sounds slick. Additionally, not everyone can be rich, and "rich" means different things to different people.

Sometimes, your career choice or other situations in your life almost guarantee you will not be wealthy beyond belief. That's okay. Being rich is no guarantee of being happy. On the other hand, I have seen plenty of people without large bank accounts who seem content.

So rather than creating my brand around the word "rich," I briefly tried a different direction and explored the word "happiness." Yes, everyone can be happy, and it isn't materialistic. However, I am a financial planner, and like it or not, I work with money. "Happiness" wasn't the right word either.

But then I had another idea—"prosperity." I loved the word because prosperity isn't limited to your money. Prosperity is also personal and involves your friends and family, your career, your pets, and activities that you enjoy. My prosperity includes my husband's, now my guardian angel's, love. I also have fabulous cats who run to meet me with meows and head butts. And I can't measure the sense of accomplishment I feel when someone understands a financial concept after I've explained it. All these good feelings are part of the prosperity I seek.

Of course, prosperity also has a financial definition. Being prosperous involves having sufficient resources to live the life you want without fear of running out of money. Financial planning has a remarkably similar definition—saving and managing financial resources in a way that helps you live your best life. More simply, your financial plan gives you a path to financial prosperity.

My wish for you is my brand: I want you to have prosperity in your life—measured in both dollars and meaningfulness. I hope this book has given you tools to help you reach your goals. If you still have a question, remember that I'm available. You can always "Ask Peggy!"

Megan: I don't have a lot of money, but Charlotte brings me extraordinary joy. You could say she makes me prosperous!

Jessica: I love the idea of being prosperous. Planning to be rich sounds a little shallow to me.

Kim: We worked with a financial adviser years ago who only focused on investment returns. There was no talk about how our money helped us live our best lives.

Sharon: The older I get, the more I realize that prosperity is actually measured in the little things. We are happiest when we focus on what brings us joy.

Next Steps

What makes you prosperous? Jot your thoughts on the following lines and then reread them during those times that life gets tough.

_____

_____

Acknowledgments

So many people helped bring 52 *Weeks to Well-Being* to life. First, heartfelt thanks to Nancy Berland. Without you, this book wouldn't exist. A chance meeting in the late 1980s changed my life, even with a thirty-year hiatus in the middle!

Next, thanks so much to Cissy Hartley and Priya Bhakta for your invaluable assistance and confidence.

Thanks, also, to everyone at Writerspace, especially Susan Simpson, for taking care of details!

On a personal note, thank you to my aunt, Margaret Beggs, who is always supportive and looking for ways to make my life easier. Thank you, also, to my family and friends who are understanding when I tell them, "I'm sorry; I can't. I'm writing."

Additionally, thank you to all the women with financial questions who worry that the financial system sees them as a marketing demographic. I hope this book provides some answers, strategies, and peace of mind. You are all queens.

Finally, thank you to my wonderful husband, Richard Doviak, who passed before 52 *Weeks to Well-Being* could be published. Sweetheart, without the wings you gave me, none of this could have happened.

About the Author

When Peggy Doviak's mother got taken to the cleaners by an unscrupulous stockbroker, Peggy got mad. She was so angry that she changed careers from corporate training to financial planning because she wanted to ensure that what happened to her mother never happened to anyone else.

Now, a best-selling personal finance author and radio host of "Ask Peggy About Your Finances," Peggy is a CERTIFIED FINANCIAL PLANNER™ practitioner and financial consumer advocate. She travels to Capitol Hill with the Financial Planning Association to promote issues including a mandatory fiduciary standard for financial professionals. She also spent fifteen years teaching CFP® certification classes and master's level courses in financial planning.

When she's not working, Peggy loves to travel, read, and spend time with her two horses and two cats.

Peggy's first book, 52 *Weeks to Prosperity*, is available through online sources or at your local bookstore. Learn more about Peggy at her website.

<u>www.askpeggy.com</u>

Made in the USA
Coppell, TX
30 September 2023

22243646R00215